D0171864

LIVING EACH DAY BY THE POWER OF FAITH

Living Each Day by the Power of Faith

Barbara Shlemon

SERVANT BOOKS
Ann Arbor, Michigan

Copyright © 1986 by Barbara Shlemon

All rights reserved.

Cover design by Michael Andaloro
Cover photo by Ed Cooper

Published by Servant Books

P.O. Box 8617
Ann Arbor, Michigan 48107

Excerpts from The Jerusalem Bible. Copyright © 1966 by
Darton, Longman & Todd, Ltd. and Doubleday & Company
Inc. Reprinted by permission of the publisher.

91 92 93 94 95   10 9 8 7 6 5 4

Printed in the United States of America

ISBN 0-89283-289-4

Contents

Preface

THE CHRISTIAN JOURNEY can be compared to modern highway travel marked with many road signs along the way; detour, yield, wrong way, merge, slow down, dangerous curve, and stop are but a few examples of the spiritual messages we often receive on the road to holiness.

Each step requires a renewed understanding of our commitment to Jesus Christ as Lord and a fresh infusion of the gift of faith. Without faith we could not travel very far on the highway of life because the road contains many obstacles which cannot be surmounted by ordinary methods. There are no maps designating each detail of the journey, so we must learn to rely on the Father's guiding hand to keep us tracking in the right direction.

Our Lord constantly challenges us to greater trust in his vigilance to watch over our comings and goings, and this is the essence of faith—trust in God's loving kindness toward his people.

The development of faith is a lifetime adventure requiring a willingness to grow in wisdom, knowledge, and understanding of the spiritual world. Each time we think the road has ended and we have finally learned to completely trust the Lord in all things, he takes us down a new path and we discover another region of uncertainty, mistrust, or fear.

Such situations give us ample opportunity to practice walking by faith, increasing our awareness of God's merciful love in the process. Like Peter, each of us is called to walk on water in a variety of religious experiences calculated to enhance trust in God. Focusing our eyes on Jesus Christ as we move through doubt, confusion, and turmoil will help our interior growth.

This book was written to assist believers in Jesus Christ to understand better the gift of faith and its role in the development of spiritual life. The first section of the book gives an overview of the components of faith, tells why it is essential to Christianity, and shows how Jesus applied faith in his ministry.

The second section of the book is designed as a month of daily meditations on various aspects of faith. Each day has a Scripture, a reflection, and a prayer to assist the reader in deepening his trust relationship with the Father in heaven. This section can be used as an individual study guide or can be easily adapted for group participation.

My hope is that as you ponder these pages you will discover many more aspects of faith and thus realize what a remarkably rich gift it is for the Body of Christ.

Part I

To Grow in Faith

ONE

Faith Means Trust

"How do I grow in faith for healing?"

So many Christians ask this question as they hear about the wonderful things God is doing in the healing ministry today. We know that faith is the key for bringing God's healing into our own lives and the lives of people dear to us. Yet we are not always sure what it means to have faith or how we can grow into a deeper faith in God's power.

During twenty-one years of involvement in the healing ministry, I have encountered people who exhort believers to "claim a healing"—whether for a physical problem, a financial need, emotional illness, or any other difficulty. I know that the Holy Spirit does sometimes inspire us to stand on the promises of Scripture with special determination and conviction. Yet often it seems that those who "claim a healing" are not acting out of specific guidance from the Holy Spirit but have made this their automatic approach to every need.

The problem with automatically claiming healings is that we can develop a dictatorial attitude, demanding that God not only give us the answer we want but also when we want it. Often, too, those who are not healed feel guilty; they assume they somehow failed to work up enough faith for God to act.

Reflecting on the words and actions of Jesus, I have come to a different understanding of faith—that it does not demand, but trusts. Jesus teaches his disciples that a tiny particle of faith is more than enough if it brings us into an attitude of reliance on God's mercy. True faith does not demand; it trusts.

Faith and Trust

Faith is the key that opens up the full riches of God's loving action in our lives. Its essence is difficult to describe because, like the virtues of love, joy, and peace, it occurs experientially.

A helpful analogy is the trapeze artist. He can swing back and forth monotonously for hours if he chooses, going nowhere. To move on to other things he must let go of his safe, comfortable bar and hang in mid-air for a moment—trusting that someone will be there to catch him before he falls to the ground. If he is tumbling in a somersault he cannot even see if someone is waiting for him; he must blindly let go of his life supports.

In order to experience faith, we have to trust that the Father will really be there when we let go of our personal securities, identities, priorities, and self-will. This looks extremely risky to us, and often we have to reach a point of desperation before we can abandon ourselves to his mercy.

I remember the Lord's gentle touch on my heart a number of years ago when I was working as a registered nurse in a small community hospital. For several months the Holy Spirit had been asking me to resign my position and wait upon God's will for my life, but I steadfastly refused to heed this "still, small voice." However, during one particularly hectic week, pressures built up that forced me to look honestly at the situation. I could no longer deny the reality of the Lord's call.

I had to make a decision. I could either throw myself on God's mercy and launch out on uncharted waters or turn away from his will completely and continue to live my life in my own way. I will never forget the fear that gripped my heart that night as I sat alone in my car in our driveway and said, "All right, I trust you with my life."

There was no indication that the Lord's arms were there to

catch me and bring instant security into my life. I felt drained as I went through the motions of handing in my resignation and trying to explain the reason to my husband and co-workers. Faith is not something we *have*; it's something we *do*. I was doing my best to put "yes" into action. The ministry of healing that developed from this exercise of trust enables me to understand the continuing importance of letting go of my way in order to come alive to his way.

This "letting go" begins when we acknowledge and nurture the love relationship between ourselves and the Father in heaven. Learning to know the tremendous depths of his all-powerful and never-failing love enables us to trust in it.

The entire Bible is a testimony to the truth of God's constant faithfulness to his promises toward those who put their trust in him. No matter how the Israelites strayed from his loving care, Yahweh was constantly reaching out to them in the words of the prophets and the action of his signs. Every promise was fulfilled in spite of the people's resistance, doubt, or fear because God is always faithful to his word. He cannot be any other way since that is his nature. "We may be unfaithful, but he is always faithful, for he cannot disown his own self" (2 Tm 2:13).

By calling us into a relationship with himself as our Father, he gives us the courage to believe in his goodness and teaches us what it means to have faith in him.

The new covenant established through Jesus Christ is a marvelous example of God's desire for relationship with his people—"Deep within them I will plant my Law, writing it on their hearts. *Then I will be their God and they shall be my people*" (Jer 31:33). It is God who initiates this reaching out to us, and, whether we respond or not, he will continually call us into a love relationship with himself because God is love.

In the beginning of our walk with the Lord, there will be many times when we doubt his love and mistrust his ability to care for us, but, if we continue to keep the lines of communication open, we will discover, as the Hebrews did, that

Yahweh is always there with loving kindness. As we experience his presence in our lives, the ability to have faith becomes activated, increasing the trust level and clarifying our understanding of the nature of God. This is not ordinarily accomplished spontaneously but, through the action of the Holy Spirit we "*learn* to know Yahweh."

The development of a trust relationship between friends requires time, patience, and perseverance. The same principles apply in the spiritual realm.

Trust is a natural outcome of healthy and loving relationships. We learn to trust a friend through years of observing his willingness to companion us through life's joys and sorrows. At some point in this journey we begin to rely on him; we start to trust the friend and stop testing his love for us. Such a relationship becomes a great source of life and gives us much courage and confidence.

Our trust level increases in the spiritual realm through these same developmental phases as we experience God's everconstant, never-changing attitude toward us. Jesus exemplified the importance of relating to the Father's love by consistently challenging his followers into ever deepening faith experiences, stretching their ability to believe in him and the Father who sent him.

He healed the sick, brought people back to life, cast out demons, and told the disciples to do likewise. As they carried out his commission, putting their faith into action, they discovered God's willingness to honor their prayers. At one time they said to Jesus, "Increase our faith . . ." and the Lord replied, "Were your faith the size of a mustard seed you could say to this mulberry tree, 'Be uprooted and planted in the sea,' and it would obey you" (Lk 17:6). Jesus taught the disciples to put into action the tiny particle of trust they already possessed.

Faith is an action word, a verb that implies doing something about our beliefs, not merely talking about them. Abraham was willing to sacrifice his son Isaac on the altar, and this is why he is called the "friend of God." The letter of James says of Abraham: "His faith became perfect by what he did" (Jas 2:22). Like Abraham our relationship with the Father is established through the action of trusting him, so it is essential that faith continue to grow through daily practice, using the tiny mustard seed of faith we already possess. Observing the Father's response to our feeble gestures of trust in him gives us courage to believe for greater things. Acting as if we have faith by carrying out daily commitments to prayer, Scripture reading, and Christian living permits the seed to grow steady and strong. We might not *feel* full of faith but we can *act* as if we are and the feelings will soon follow.

Sometimes we fail to develop a strong trust in the Father's willingness to answer our prayers because we take on prayer projects too large for our faith level. When the desired results are not forthcoming, we interpret this to mean God has rejected our petitions and we cease trying to understand his will. Listening to the prayers of intercession in our churches on Sunday morning, I often wonder how many persons in the congregation really believe the Father is going to stop the war in Northern Ireland, solve the abortion issue, or return all the missing children as a direct result of our petitions. These problems are so overwhelming that the most we can do is answer, "Lord, hear our prayer," with very little enthusiasm.

Since our faith level is built on experience, we need to receive answers to our prayers before we can wholeheartedly enter into intercessory prayer. Therefore, in the initial stages of growth in faith, it is best to choose prayer projects which are not too great for our faith level to accommodate. Acute illnesses, small burns, cuts, bruises, or abrasions generally demonstrate dramatic response to prayer, thus increasing confidence in our ability to channel God's healing love. Rearing five active children provided me with numerous opportunities to pray for minor accidents and illnesses normal to family life. Many times we watched as bruises disappeared or severe cuts stopped bleeding immediately when we began to pray. These experiences did much to encourage the children to trust in the Father's concern for them and certainly expanded my trust in his protection over us.

Occasionally prayer groups are criticized for spending time interceding for mundane things, but these exercises enable the mustard seed of faith to grow and produce a great harvest. During the morning of a healing prayer workshop, I instructed the participants to choose one prayer project for that day which they believed could be accomplished through their intercessions. Later a Protestant minister shared his experience in praying for his infected and swollen thumb. He said, "Maybe a hangnail on the thumb is not a big deal for most people, but I am a concert organist and have been unable to practice due to this infection. As soon as I began to pray for this situation, the pain and swelling immediately subsided, and my thumb was no longer sore to the touch. I know that I'm only at the 'hangnail stage of faith' right now, but I fully expect to be able to believe God for even greater things as a result of this workshop."

Faith in God's Goodness

Repeatedly throughout the gospels, Jesus shows that faith in God means believing in the Father's goodness and in his willingness to bring abundant life to us. "If you, then, who are evil know how to give your children what is good, how much more will your Father in heaven give good things to those who ask him!" (Mt 7:11). When Jesus tells us to have faith in God he is calling us to an attitude of trust in the providence of a loving creator who wants only the best for his creation.

Mark's Gospel relates the story of a father who brought his epileptic son to the disciples (see Mk 9:17-29). They were unable to cure the boy. When Jesus arrived on the scene he confronted the father with the challenging statement,

"Everything is possible for anyone who has faith." Immediately the father of the boy cried out, "I do have faith. Help the little faith I have" (Mk 9:24).

Until the father verbalized this statement, Jesus did nothing to heal this child who had been tormented from the time he was a little toddler. According to the father's report, he frequently had uncontrollable attacks which even threw him into the fire. Perhaps this father had developed too protective an attitude toward his son during the years he cared for him in his affliction. When a parent's healthy protective instinct turns to fear, it can erect unconscious barriers to the Lord's power. Jesus forced the father to abandon control of the situation and to trust in him to care for the child. The father's honesty in admitting that his faith was very small illustrates how difficult it must have been to let go and let God be in charge. Nevertheless, Jesus did not respond to the degree of the father's faith but to his expression of his faith.

It is interesting to note that Jesus did not in any way elicit an expression of belief from the child. This is counter to the current "claim your healing" teachings. The burden for the faith response was placed on the father and his openness to God's action in his son's life. This provides an excellent illustration of relinquishment of our loved ones into the hands of Jesus Christ who loves them even more than we do.

God's healing is severely hampered when we are unwilling to trust him to do the most loving thing for us or our loved ones. Family members and close friends become beautiful channels of blessings as they learn to entrust everything into the care of the one who created us.

I have observed numerous instances of dramatic changes in the physical condition of ill children or spouses following this prayer of relinquishment: "Lord, Jesus Christ, I entrust (son, daughter, husband, wife, mother, etc.) into your care for I believe that you love (him/her) more than I do." If possible, it is helpful to envision the loved one in the arms of Jesus who abundantly transmits the Father's love.

Interceding Out of Trust

When our relationship to the Father in heaven is founded on trust, our intercessory prayers are more effective. If we perceive God as an all-powerful deity whose will is harsh and judgmental, prayer becomes an attempt to persuade him to be kind and generous. We are inwardly fearful of his will, so we pray tense, pleading petitions. We seem to think that if we pray long enough, hard enough, and loud enough, God will relent and not bring wrath down upon us.

The heart that trusts can pray as Jesus did at the tomb of his friend Lazarus: "Father, I thank you for hearing my prayer. I knew indeed that you always hear me" (Jn 11:41-42). If there were ever a circumstance that needed intensive, concentrated prayer, this was it! Lazarus was dead four days, and Jesus knew he was to call him back to this life. Yet there was no pleading, no demanding, no telling God what to do. Jesus simply stated belief in the divine presence; he thanked his Father for always being with him and always hearing his prayer. He trusted the Father to act in the most loving way regarding Lazarus and his family. The prayer reflected confidence in the goodness of God and in his willingness to meet the needs of his people.

Jesus could realize this degree of faith because he was aware of all the ways God had blessed him in the past and was therefore confident the Father would continue to manifest care, compassion, and concern. This was in keeping with the Jewish tradition of constantly remembering their salvation history, recalling the mighty works of Yahweh in order to maintain proper perspective during times of stress and trial. Jesus refused to be influenced by the situation at hand but chose instead to bring to mind the powerful ways the Father was always present to him. In so doing his faith remained active, and a great miracle occurred!

Sometimes we fail to recognize the mercy of the Father because we ask him the wrong question regarding circumstances in our lives. The Lord will seldom answer the query,

"Why did this happen to me?" and we can waste many precious moments of prayer time by demanding to understand why. God's ways are not our ways, and attempting to comprehend his mysterious methods often leads to frustration.

Instead of seeking reasons for the Father's ways, we can discover greater benefits for growth in faith by changing the question to, "What good happened as a result of this development?" or "How is my life richer because God did not respond to my prayer as I anticipated?" Such questions nearly always promote a new vision of the Lord's goodness and deeper trust in his ability to care for us.

Remembering the Hard Times Too

Recently a woman scheduled for surgery to correct a deteriorating heart condition traveled to Florida for vacation. During her visit she attended a healing service at Our Lady of Divine Providence House of Prayer, where several staff members prayed for her. She told them that her physical symptoms had appeared the previous year, soon after the death of her husband. Her physician was convinced that the problem was related to stress.

Throughout her husband's illness this woman and her prayer group had interceded for his healing and had received scriptural confirmation that he would be healed. His death created feelings of anger and bitterness toward the Lord and caused her to stop attending prayer meetings. The constant question, "Why did this happen?" brought no comfort.

Gently our staff members asked the woman to rephrase the question, "What good happened as a result of this situation?" Initially she was unable to discover any positive results, but after quiet pondering she began to recognize growth areas.

The husband's death had reunited their previously separated family. All five children were now in good relationship with the mother and with the Lord. She had gained a new ability to confront financial matters, which had always confused her. Most importantly, she became aware that God's promise to heal her husband was fulfilled with his entrance into heaven, where God "will wipe away all tears from their eyes; there will be no more death, and no more mourning or sadness" (Rv 21:4).

When the woman returned home her physical condition had improved so much that her doctor cancelled the surgery.

Faith is strengthened as we invite the Father to reveal the beneficial results of pain and suffering. The world refuses to accept the value of the cross, but Jesus teaches us to look beyond it to the joy of resurrection.

Growing in Trust

Believing that God is good and wants only good things for us creates an attitude of trust in his sovereign action. Our personal vision is extremely narrow, because we see through a dark glass, but the heavenly Father has a more comprehensive viewpoint. Capturing the essence of God's loving nature helps us believe that "by turning everything to their good, God co-operates with all those who love him, with all those that he has called according to his purpose" (Rom 8:28).

The following pages contain a month of daily meditations designed to foster a deeper faith relationship with the Father. We recognize faith as a gift of the Holy Spirit, yet we can encourage development of this gift through a variety of methods. Faith has numerous components. I have only touched on a few, but implementing these will help you grow in trust.

Before beginning each section, invite the Holy Spirit to reveal what he desires you to learn from the exercises. Be willing to look at areas of inadequacy, unhealthy habit patterns, and walls of resistance in regard to trusting the Lord. He longs to bring us closer to his heart but the key to open the door is within our being.

Faith is a daily exercise of trust. Peter explained it very beautifully in his first letter to the early Christians: "Through your faith, God's power will guard you until the salvation which has been prepared is revealed at the end of time. This is a cause of great joy for you, even though you may for a short time have to bear being plagued by all sorts of trials; so that, when Jesus Christ is revealed, your faith will have been tested and proved like gold" (1 Pt 1:5-7).

Part II

To Walk in Faith: Daily Meditations

Each meditation should be preceded by a prayer to the Holy Spirit, inviting God's wisdom to penetrate the mystery of faith and to permit increased understanding of this virtue.

Prayer to Begin Meditating on Faith

Come, Holy Spirit, enlighten my mind to comprehend the mystery of the gift of faith and its meaning for my life. Assist me to integrate this virtue more deeply into my spiritual, emotional, and physical development so that I may become faith-filled in my journey toward holiness. Thank you for opening my heart to receive this important instrument of growth. Give me continued reliance on your light to strengthen my trust relationship with my Father in heaven.

TWO

Faith Means Freedom from Fear

The spirit you received is not the spirit of slaves bringing fear into your lives again; it is the spirit of sons, and it makes us cry out, "Abba, Father!" (Rom 8:14-15)

THE MODERN WORLD APPEARS TO BE permeated with fears concerning the future of this planet Earth. Constant bombardment by news media reports of wars, violence, and murder has raised the stress level to such a degree that even young children are adversely affected. One mother of an eight-year-old daughter told of hearing the child crying in her bedroom because, "We're all going to die in a nuclear war." Teachers tell of children discussing their future with the phrase, "*If* I grow up . . ." not "*When* I grow up . . ." as it was expressed in previous generations.

Stress among teenagers is demonstrated by the alarming statistic that the primary causes of death in their age group are auto accidents and suicide.

The fear response in the adult population is no less intense as we drown our anxieties in a sea of alcohol, drugs, and other destructive things. Physicians estimate the majority of patients in their waiting rooms are suffering from psychosomatic illness—the wear and tear of the mind on the body.

The Scriptures have much to say on this subject as Jesus continually exhorted those around him to be not afraid but trust in the Father's protective love. Luke's Gospel contains a passage which clearly states the kind of faith which Jesus expects from his followers.

"To you my friends I say: Do not be afraid of those who kill the body and after that can do no more. I will tell you whom to fear: fear him who, after he has killed, has the power to cast into hell. Yes, I tell you, fear him. Can you not buy five sparrows for two pennies? And yet not one is forgotten in God's sight. Why every hair on your head has been counted. There is no need to be afraid: you are worth more than hundreds of sparrows." (Lk 12:4-7)

Freedom from fear becomes a reality when we recognize that our lives belong to a creator who will not abandon us to the powers of evil. Through the death and resurrection of Jesus Christ we have eternal life in the Father's kingdom. Unless we really believe this truth, we will have much difficulty relating to the heavenly Father in a trusting way. Our faith in him means we cannot allow fear to paralyze us or cause us to doubt his ability to watch over us and our loved ones.

Some time ago, television presented a dramatic enactment of the aftermath of nuclear disaster, "The Day After." Prior to the telecast we were warned about the frightening aspects of the presentation and literally psyched-up for anxiety reactions which many persons experienced. One mother told me her teenage daughter was terrified and unable to attend school for several days following the showing.

Recently Bishop Nelson Litwiller of the Mennonite Church shared an interesting insight about that program. During the scenes of destruction he noted the background music was the old and well-known Protestant hymn, "How Firm a Foundation." The words of this hymn taken from Isaiah 43 are extremely comforting whether or not the producers of the show chose it deliberately. Regardless of the rationale, the Holy Spirit was giving a strong subliminal message of hope to all the viewers of the program.

How Firm A Foundation
by Richard Keen

How firm a foundation, ye saints of the Lord,
Is laid for your faith in His excellent Word!
What more can he say than to you He hath said,
To you who for refuge to Jesus have fled?

"Fear not, I am with thee, O be not dismayed;
For I am thy God and will still give thee aid.
I'll strengthen thee, help thee, and cause thee to stand,
Upheld by my righteous, omnipotent hand.

When through the deep waters I will call thee to go,
The rivers of sorrow shall not overflow.
For I will be with thee, thy troubles to bless,
And sanctify to thee thy deepest distress.

When through fiery trials thy pathway shall lie,
My grace, all-sufficient, shall be thy supply.
The flame shall not hurt thee, I only design
Thy dross to consume, and thy gold to refine.

The soul that on Jesus hath leaned for repose,
I will not, I will not desert to his foes,
That soul, though all hell should endeavor to shake,
I'll never, no never, no never forsake!"

*

Dear Jesus, I have allowed the world to undermine faith in you and in your Father by permitting fear of the future to permeate my thoughts and decisions. Please help me to recognize the magnitude of the goodness of my God who does not desire destruction of this earth but transformation into the new earth. Consume my fears with the fire of your love so I may continually radiate hope to those around me, thus witnessing to the faith I have in your saving Presence. Thank you for being a Father who can be trusted to care for me and for my loved ones.

THREE

Faith Means Perseverance

Now will not God see justice done to his chosen who cry to him day and night even when he delays to help them? I promise you, he will see justice done to them, and done speedily. But when the son of man comes, will he find any faith on earth? (Lk 18:6-8)

JESUS TELLS THE PARABLE OF A WIDOW who needed to resolve a dispute and approached a town official for assistance (Lk 18:1-8). The Lord characterizes this judge as having "no fear of God nor respect for man," so it seems safe to conclude he misused his position. Judges were accorded a great deal of political power but were generally regarded as publicans and sinners because they depended on bribes for their living. Even today in many Eastern lands it is customary to send a bribe prior to visiting a judge in order to obtain a hearing. Arriving at the judge's door without the advanced payment indicates they are poor and the servants are instructed to send them away.

However, the widow in Jesus' story continually approached the judge saying, "I want justice from you against my enemy." For a long time he ignored her plea but finally relented by reasoning, "since she keeps pestering me I must give this widow her just rights, or she will persist in coming and worrying me to death."

The Lord compares the heavenly Father with the wicked

judge and points out that if such a corrupt man finally gives a hearing, the gracious God is even more eager to "see justice done to his chosen who cry out to him day and night, *even when he delays to help them.*"

The parable is meant to encourage us to pray constantly and never lose heart when seeking justice for ourselves and others. The widow exercised great faith by believing that even this dishonest politician would, eventually, permit truth to triumph. The Father in heaven is neither dishonest nor corrupt, therefore we can demonstrate trust in him by continuing to seek the answers to our petitions even when he apparently delays to send them.

I believe the Lord sometimes withholds the answers we are seeking in order to increase our faith. If all prayer petitions were automatically granted, would we have opportunities for exercising trust? We would have never heard of St. Monica if the Father converted her son, Augustine, through the uttering of her first intercessions on his behalf. Through forty years of tears and supplications she and her son became sanctified by the practice of perseverance in prayer. Perhaps the Lord doesn't spontaneously respond to our petitions for husbands, wives, or children because he desires sainthood for us by this same method!

For ten years I prayed for my husband to be converted to the Catholic faith and baptized in the Holy Spirit. Many times during those years I agonized in prayer and argued with God over his long delay in granting my request. When my husband finally received the gift of faith in 1974, it was a great and glorious day made doubly joyful because of the many years of knocking at the Father's door. In retrospect, I realize how much my faith was tested and increased due to God's wisdom in waiting. I learned to trust in him even when the results were not obvious and this can be real in-service training for growth.

Often we become weary in praying for a particular request and cease knocking on the door of the Father's house. Our society is accustomed to instant coffee, microwave ovens, and express lanes so we easily lose patience when we have to wait for anything. A thirty minute delay in the departure of an airplane can trigger almost barbaric behavior as passengers experience the frustration of waiting. We are personally offended by anything that causes us to slow down from the frantic rush of our daily lives.

However, the heavenly kingdom is not geared toward the timetable of earth—in God's sight a thousand years are as a day. What seems interminable to us is but a blink of the eye to God. For centuries Christians have been looking for the return of Jesus Christ, longing for him to bring in the new heaven and new earth, but he does not appear to be in any hurry to fulfill the book of Revelation.

Delay in answering our petitions teaches us to trust him even when results are not in evidence. Seeking, asking, and knocking does not have to be frustrating if we recognize it is an opportunity to grow in the virtue of patience.

The story of the importunate widow encourages us to exercise faith through continued prayer.

*

Lord, Jesus Christ, grant me the grace of faithful perseverance in prayer that I may pray constantly and never lose heart. Help me to be patient in waiting for the answers with hopeful expectations of the outcome. Let not despair and hopelessness cause me to mistrust your love but enable me to believe in your goodness even when you seemingly delay in answering my petitions. I ask for the grace to continually put my trust in you, daily bringing my intentions before you. Please help me to grow in faith through this exercise of prayerful perseverance.

FOUR

Faith Means Good Works

*I tell you most solemnly, whoever believes in me will perform the
same works I do myself, he will perform even greater works,
because I am going to the Father.* (Jn 14:12)

"Take the case, my brothers, of someone who has never done
a single good act but claims that he has faith. Will that faith
save him? If one of the brothers or one of the sisters is in need
of clothes and has not enough food to live on, and one of you
says to them, 'I wish you well; keep yourself warm and eat
plenty,' without giving them these bare necessities of life, then
what good is that? Faith is like that: if good works do not go
with it, it is quite dead" (Jas 2:14-16).

James is quite explicit in reminding Christians to express
their faith in Jesus Christ through some type of service to
others, or it will be rendered useless. Opening our hearts in a
faith relationship to the Lord should make us more sensitive to
the needs of those around us, and make us more generous than
we were previously. Believing in Jesus Christ brings salvation
and eternal life in his kingdom. Reaching out to others actively
demonstrates this inner commitment.

Jesus called his followers the light of the world and stated,
"Your light must shine in the sight of men, so that, *seeing your
good works,* they may give praise to your Father in heaven" (Mt

33

5:16). The Christian life is designed to light up the world through good works because this is a radical departure from the selfishness, greed, and lack of love in society. Christians are expected to be socially visible—not because we constantly talk about the Lord, but because our lives reflect his inner presence through the charity we exhibit.

Mahatma Gandhi challenged us with the statement that he would have become a Christian if he had ever met one. Undoubtedly he encountered hundreds of Christians in his many years of travel, but never discovered one who lived out a radical commitment to Jesus Christ in generous service to others. Perhaps if he had lived long enough to meet Mother Teresa, his opinion would have been altered, but his admonition is still valid for most of us who call ourselves Christian. We need to be willing to share time, talent, and treasure as a sign of our fellowship with our Lord. In so doing, our faith is strengthened through imitation of the personality of Jesus Christ, who constantly gave all that he had into the Father's service.

This type of behavior provides a strong witness in today's world. Studies indicate that the central reason people join religious cults is because, initially, these organizations reached out to them with food, clothing, and financial assistance and drew them into what appeared to be a loving community atmosphere. For example, the Church of Scientology headquartered in Clearwater, Florida, regularly recruits new members through a constant campaign to find jobs for the unemployed.

Most Christian churches administrate programs which assist the needy, but very few members of the congregation are actively involved in what used to be called corporate works of mercy. By avoiding such works we not only negate our profession of faith but also deny ourselves many blessings. "Give, and there will be gifts for you: a full measure, pressed down, shaken together, and running over, will be poured into your lap; because the amount you measure out is the amount you will be given back" (Lk 6:38).

God's economic principles are different from the world's banking methods. Jesus tells us to give of ourselves, our time, and our money if we want to receive anything in return. One elderly gentleman told his prayer group that he had searched for inner peace all his life, trying every possible method of fulfillment, i.e., travel, career changes, material acquisitions. At age seventy-two he became involved in the meals on wheels program to the shut-ins of his community and discovered the key which unlocked the treasure house of spiritual blessings. "I've never been so happy nor felt so fulfilled," he said.

Sharing finances with those less fortunate is a certain guarantee the Father will generously care for our needs. The principle of tithing, giving a tenth of our money to the Lord, is as valid today as in the early Christian church. For many years I misunderstood this teaching and failed to receive many blessings from the Lord. We had barely enough income to cover our expenses so I did not think the Father expected me to give anything to the church. Finally, someone pointed me to a passage in Malachi where Yahweh says, "Bring the full tithes and dues to the storehouse . . . and then see if I do not open the floodgates of heaven for you and pour out blessing for you in abundance" (Mal 3:10). God didn't increase our finances if I didn't give him something to multiply.

The Father we serve will not be outdone in generosity. When I finally let go of our finances and placed them in the hands of the Lord, he showed me that he was a much better money manager than I could ever be. When our daughter, Beth, was struggling to balance her checking account in the early stages of learning to live on her own, I told her Jesus' teaching to give and it will be given back. She was elated to report, "It really works! Whenever I can't meet my bills, I give something away and the Lord provides."

The principle of demonstrating faith through good works is an essential spiritual exercise for building trust in the Father's care for us.

*

Heavenly Father, I ask you to forgive my sins of omission in failing to reach out to a brother or sister in need. Often I have allowed selfishness to rule my life and have been oblivious to the sufferings of others. Please help me to willingly become more generous with my time. Let me not become irritated when personal plans are disrupted by someone who needs to talk or who needs a ride to the doctor or a shoulder to cry on. Grant me the grace to joyfully share my material goods and finances as a sign of trust in your ability to meet my own needs. May the good works of my life truly bring glory to my Father in heaven like a light shining in the darkness.

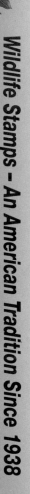

Wildlife Stamps – An American Tradition Since 1938

They bring the beauty and wonder of America's wildlife to the Christmas season, and show the wildlife heritage we are working for. When you use these Stamps on your cards and gifts, you're showing your concern for wildlife and conservation as you help us work for a healthier environment.

© 1991 National Wildlife Federation • 1400 Sixteenth Street, N.W. • Washington, D.C. 20036-2266

Working for the Nature of Tomorrow®

Note: You are under no obligation to pay for or donate in response to receiving these Stamps, but your support is important to us.

E5104

These Christmas Stamps Do a Wonderful Job!

FIVE

Faith Means Honesty with God

Cry, and Yahweh will answer;
call, and he will say, "I am here."

If you do away with the yoke,
the clenched fist, the wicked word,
if you give your bread to the hungry,
and relief to the oppressed,

your light will rise in the darkness,
and your shadows become like noon.
Yahweh will always guide you,
giving you relief in desert places. (Is 58:9-11)

ANGER TOWARD THE HEAVENLY FATHER is not an unusual emotion for Christians to experience. He is the creator of the universe, the almighty and everlasting God who sees and knows all things, and we resent his apparent lack of compassion.

"If God is all-loving why are babies born handicapped, why do we have earthquakes, why is there no end to war in the world?" are questions voiced in our hearts and sometimes on our lips. Occasionally we have felt disillusioned or disappointed in relating to the Lord because certain prayer requests were not answered in the way we had hoped.

Most Christians do a good job of suppressing the angry emotions felt toward God, they believe acknowledgment of them would be blasphemy or would indicate a sinful heart or a lack of faith. However, since faith really means developing a trust relationship with the Father, it is vitally important to willingly share all our thoughts and feelings with him. The truth is that God already knows what is in our heart. We need to admit these attitudes to ourselves in an open and honest way for they can obstruct spiritual growth.

Moses is a marvelous example of one who wasn't afraid to "tell it like it is" in his conversations with God. The Israelites began to grumble about their unhappy circumstances in the desert and "Moses heard the people wailing, every family at the door of its tent. . . . He spoke to Yahweh: 'Why do you treat your servant so badly? Why have I not found favor with you, so that you load on me the weight of all this nation? . . . I am not able to carry this nation by myself alone; the weight is too much for me. If this is how you want to deal with me, I would rather you killed me! If only I had found favor in your eyes, and not lived to see such misery as this!' " (Nm 11:11-15).

Yahweh does not rebuke Moses for his insolence but, instead, tells him to gather seventy of the elders into the Tent of Meeting. "I will come down to speak with you; and I will take some of the spirit which is on you and put it on them. So they will share with you the burden of this nation, and you will no longer have to carry it by yourself" (Nm 11:16-17). It was as if the Lord was waiting for Moses to finally admit his frustrations in leading the Israelites. As long as he was suppressing all these feelings, the door wasn't open for the Father to pour out his blessings on the Israelites.

Tevye, the Jewish milkman in *Fiddler on the Roof,* is another example of someone who wasn't afraid to speak to God about everything in his heart. His prayer conversations complain about his lame horse, his poverty, his rebellious daughters, but always in a spirit of reverence toward the creator. This attitude marks the difference between those whose anger is self-righteous and the person who sincerely desires to grow in the love of the Lord. Ventilating emotions toward the Father promotes a deepening in the relationship if we are willing to let God be God in the governing of his universe, "for my thoughts are not your thoughts, my ways not your ways ..." (Is 55:8). Sharing our inner feelings does not give us license to dictate to God; it simply brings to the light what is hidden, allowing the Father to do with it as he wills.

Several years ago I was in a period of extreme frustration trying to fulfill my responsibilities as wife and mother to five teenagers along with trying to meet the demands of an active healing ministry. At one point I felt as if the entire weight of everyone's problems was on my back, and in desperation I sat in the back of church one afternoon pouring out my anger. "Lord, I can't keep going this way or I will break. Why are you expecting so much from me?"

The next day I received a phone call from a woman who was moving into the Clearwater area and who wanted to know if she could help me with my secretarial work. She assisted me in numerous ways, taking on much of the administrative work and freeing me to spend more time with my family. Until I finally let go of all that inner turmoil, the answers to my needs were not forthcoming.

Confronting feelings of disappointment and admitting them to ourselves and to God can allow the light of his Spirit to give us a new perspective on the situation. Clearing the channels enables us to realize how much the Father loves us and does not will darkness and destruction. Putting on the mind of Christ regarding our lives means we have to give up our old way of thinking, and this process is often facilitated through talking to God in an open and honest manner, just as Moses discovered.

*

Dear Father, there are times I have doubted your loving care for me, my loved ones, and the world. I see suffering and pain and wonder at your apparent apathy. I sometimes feel anger toward you for not answering prayers or granting blessings the way I want you to. Since you "know my heart," I admit these feelings to you and to myself. Please help me to see the truth through your eyes and to trust you even when I don't understand your ways. Grant me inner peace in the midst of my trials and struggles, the peace that passes understanding. Heal my heart of its sorrow regarding disappointments in relating to you . . . the times when I didn't accept your action in my life. Thank you for being a Father who allows me to be open with my feelings. May this honesty give me new freedom to trust in your compassionate love today and always.

SIX

Faith Means Action

*Everyone who comes to me and listens to my words and acts on
them—I will show you what he is like. He is like the man who
when he built his house dug, and dug deep, and laid the
foundations on rock; when the river was in flood it bore down on
that house but could not shake it, it was like the man who built
his house on soil, with no foundations: as soon as the river bore
down on it, it collapsed; and what a ruin that
house became!* (Lk 6:47-49)

FAITH IS NOT SOMETHING WE HAVE but something we do.
Putting the smallest degree of trust into some type of action
begins to increase the little faith we have, generating wider and
deeper belief in the Father's care.

Everyone demonstrates faith in one way or another through
daily encountering situations which require trust. Turning on
the light switch, we trust the power company will provide the
proper amount of energy to activate the bulb. Opening a can of
beans, we believe the label means what it says and that the food
is not contaminated.

We travel on planes confident the pilot will take us to our
destination. Most persons would feel foolish demanding the
pilot constantly reassure the passengers of their safety. We
learn to trust the airlines by allowing ourselves to experience
air travel even when, initially, we may feel skeptical or fearful.

We must utilize a mustard seed of faith by walking onto the airplane.

No matter how much we think we lack faith in our lives, it has to be operating in some manner or we would be forced to endure total isolation from the rest of humanity.

Just as faith is demonstrated through action in daily living, so it needs to be activated in our spiritual lives. We don't wait until we feel high intensity of faith towards the Father. Such confidence generally develops after the fact. We begin by utilizing the little mustard seed already within our hearts, planting it by acknowledging its existence.

The father of the epileptic child in Mark's Gospel demonstrated faith in something outside of himself when he brought his son to the disciples of Jesus for healing. His action spoke louder than the words, "I do have faith, help the little faith I have," for without his prior conduct the words would have been meaningless. The Scriptures cite numerous situations in which Jesus commends persons for their faith because they came to him, not because of what they *said* to him. In Nazareth, they believed he was the carpenter's son so they didn't bring their sick to him for healing. He was unable to work miracles there, and "he was amazed at their lack of faith" (Mk 6:6).

In our daily lives we can exercise faith in God by attending church service, receiving the Sacraments, joining a prayer group or Scripture study, reading spiritual literature, taking time out from the busyness of our day to talk to the Lord. Many times these procedures are not accompanied by a great feeling of faith but as we continue to keep the door of our hearts open, the Holy Spirit starts to make a way for faith to become more operative. When we come to the Lord, acknowledging through our actions that we believe in him, even when we don't feel so inclined, the Father more than meets us halfway. Kathryn Kuhlman estimated that nearly forty percent of persons healed during her miracle service had not accepted Jesus Christ as Savior, yet they were touched by his healing power simply because they came to the services.

Several years ago I was a member of a team invited to minister in India. The majority of those thousands who attended the large outdoor rallies were Hindus, and it was not at all unusual for them to be healed of very serious physical problems, i.e., blindness, deafness, paralysis. It was interesting to talk with them after the services and discover that although many had never even heard the name of Jesus Christ, he touched them because they came to him. We were able to lead many to accept Jesus as Lord and Savior through this outpouring of his love.

Is there some way you can demonstrate faith in action today?

Have you been waiting for God to make the first move, failing to realize he is patiently waiting for you to open the door of your heart?

Don't look at your feeling, your sense of unworthiness, your doubts and fears, but move toward his love in some tangible, concrete expression of belief in him.

*

Dear Jesus, forgive me for ignoring you by not putting the little faith that I do have into some kind of action. Help me to overcome any stubbornness, obstinacy, or laziness which keeps me from going to church, reading your Word, or fellowshipping with other believers. Give me the courage to practice trusting in you by regularly approaching you through the channels of prayer, Scripture reading, and the sacramental life. I promise to act in a faithful manner toward you, thus opening the door to receive a greater awareness of your presence in my life. Please teach me the meaning of faith.

SEVEN

Faith Means Testing

My dear people, you must not think it unaccountable that you should be tested by fire. There is nothing extraordinary in what has happened to you. If you can have some share in the sufferings of Christ, be glad, because you will enjoy a much greater gladness when his glory is revealed. (1 Pt 4:12-13)

My son, if you aspire to serve the Lord, / prepare yourself for an ordeal. / Be sincere of heart, be steadfast, / and do not be alarmed when disaster comes. / Cling to him and do not leave him, / so that you may be honored at the end of your days. / Whatever happens to you, accept it, / and in the uncertainties of your humble state, be patient, / since gold is tested in the fire, / and chosen men in the furnace of humiliation. (Eccl 2:1-5)

THIS PASSAGE FROM THE OLD TESTAMENT should be required reading for anyone who is contemplating answering the call of God for ministry and service. "If you aspire to serve the Lord, prepare yourself for an ordeal." As this Scripture clearly indicates, following the will of the Father does not guarantee freedom from trials, problems, and sufferings. Developing a trust relationship with God brings countless opportunities to exercise faith so it can become a normal part of our spiritual lives.

Faith never put to the test is weak and ineffectual; therefore the Lord provides many ways of strengthening spiritual muscles so we can "run and not be weary, walk and not faint." The analogy of an athlete in training graphically illustrates the methods employed by the Lord to build up our inner resources so we can withstand the devil's temptations.

The story of Abraham's willingness to sacrifice his son Isaac is a well-known example of someone whose faith in God was strengthened through a very difficult trial. The Father may never ask us to endure anything quite so challenging; Abraham's faith was already very strong, so only a most extreme trial could test it. St. Paul explains the process to the Corinthians: "The trials that you have had to bear are no more than people normally have. You can trust God not to let you be tried beyond your strength, and with any trial he will give you a way out of it and the strength to bear it" (1 Cor 10:13).

Paul tells the early Christians to expect problems and difficulties as a normal part of spiritual development, not a sign of God's disfavor. Often we interpret times of trial as a punishment: "If God is love why do I have suffering in my life?" One result of such thinking is acceptance of a heavy burden of guilt which greatly compounds the situation. The friends of Job worked very hard to prove his sins were the cause of his pain, but freedom came when he stopped condemning himself and started trusting in God's goodness.

Recognizing tribulation as a normal part of Christian growth and not as divine retribution can do much to offset negative thinking and increase our faith in God. An incident in the life of St. Teresa of Avila is an amusing but helpful illustration. She felt guided by the Holy Spirit to visit her sisters in various convents throughout Spain. The weather was cold, windy, and rainy during most of the journey, and while stepping from the coach, she fell face down into the muddy water. Cold, wet, and dirty, she cried out, "If this is how you treat your friends, no wonder you have so few!"

Sometimes it seems we have more problems in our lives after we become Christians than before, making it imperative that we gain the Lord's perspective on this dilemma. At one time Jesus said to Peter, "Simon, Simon! Satan, you must know, has got his wish to sift you all like wheat; but I have prayed for you, Simon, that your faith may not fail, and once you have recovered, you in your turn must strengthen your brother" (Lk 22:31). In order to prepare them for the conflict, Jesus was warning Peter of the sufferings he and the other disciples would soon face. Forewarned is forearmed. If we expect our relationship with the Father to be filled with consolation, we are definitely unprepared for the desolation. Jesus wanted Peter to understand that the road ahead would be marked with many trials calculated to increase his faith so that he could be an instrument for strengthening others.

As we learn to trust the Father through times of sorrow and pain, he calls us to assist others during their trials. For example, a person who has endured the death of a loved one can be a rich source of encouragement to someone with a similar problem. Our deepest suffering can eventually become a gift from God which confers deep faith in his abiding presence.

The struggles we encounter in our walk with the Lord provide us with opportunities to experience his power to keep us from breaking under their weight. Usually we are unaware of God's keeping until the storm passes, but when it's over we can look back and see that he was always there.

*

Dear Jesus, forgive me for doubting your presence during times of trial and tribulation when I didn't always *feel* your consoling love. You promised to always be with me, but I sometimes despair of your help or become fearful that you will desert me in the chaos and confusion of crisis periods. Help me not to burden myself with false guilt when the dark times come. Enable me to look up to you and believe you will never leave me. Give me the courage to stand firm in the face of turmoil, secure in the promises you have made to all who believe in you. Grant me the wisdom to see good coming from every situation, no matter how disastrous it may seem at the time. Thank you for the ordeals which expand my faith and allow me to trust you more each day.

EIGHT

Faith Means Forgiving

And forgive us our debts, as we have forgiven those who are in debt to us . . . . Yes, if you forgive others their failing, your heavenly Father will forgive you yours; but if you do not forgive others, your Father will not forgive your failings either. (Mt 6:11, 14-15)

TRUST IN THE LORD can grow through the practice of forgiving others since we cannot approach the throne of God with an open and yielded heart if we are holding on to resentments, hurt feelings, and bitterness. "And when you stand in prayer, forgive whatever you have against anybody, so that your Father in heaven may forgive your failings too" (Mk 11:25). Forgiving those who hurt us is a primary component of faith because unforgiveness greatly affects our relationship with the Father. Jesus repeatedly taught his disciples the necessity of forgiving whatever we have against anybody. Right order in the Father's kingdom means that we cannot expect to receive forgiveness if we are unwilling to give it.

Twenty years of experience in healing prayer ministry has convinced me there is nothing which blocks our ability to be blessed by the Father's love more than unwillingness to forgive. This attitude erects strong barriers to receiving God's grace for physical, emotional, and spiritual healing. A recent newspaper article told of two brothers in Massachusetts who died within two hours of each other. For twenty-five years they had split the family with a feud caused by a long forgotten disagreement. The feud ended when they both died of heart attacks in the same hospital emergency room, with the same attendants on the same day. The bitterness against one another had been so great, that it had prevented them from visiting their ailing mother because neither wanted to encounter the other at her bedside. They died without ever reconciling the situation and left much brokenness and sorrow in their households.

This type of stubbornness is not uncommon, even among Christians who often find many excuses for holding on to resentments and hurt feelings. Jesus frequently reminded the disciples that forgiving those who wronged them was a condition of being a true follower of his. Peter evidently had difficulty with this teaching because at one point he questioned the Lord, " 'How often must I forgive my brother if he wrongs me? As often as seven times?' Jesus answered, 'Not seven I tell you, but seventy-seven times' " (Mt 18:19). Peter wanted a specific number, but Jesus responded with a deliberately inflated figure which conveyed an infinite amount because forgiveness is never-ending if we truly desire fellowship with the Father.

During his death on the cross, Jesus demonstrated the importance of forgiveness when he cried, "Father, forgive them, they do not know what they are doing." In the midst of excruciating pain, he looked at the crowd demanding his crucifixion and refused to allow resentment and bitterness into his heart. There were undoubtedly many in that group who had received healings from Jesus and had listened to his teachings, yet they were caught up in the mob which desired his death. Jesus had the power to retaliate by calling thousands of his angels to avenge him, but he chose the way of forgiveness. Through this example, the Lord reminds us to imitate his behavior and not permit the root of bitterness to prevent growth in the Holy Spirit.

The parable of the unforgiving debtor emphasizes that failure to pardon others keeps them as well as us imprisoned in some manner. The master in this story cancelled his servant's debt of ten thousand talents (an extremely large sum of money) when he asked for mercy. But the servant did not respond with similar kindness toward his fellow servant who owed him a relatively small debt of one hundred denarii but had him jailed until payment was rendered. This so angered the master that he ordered the unforgiving servant to be "handed over to the torturers until he should pay all his debt. And that is how my heavenly Father will deal with you unless you each forgive your brother from your heart" (Mt 18:23-35).

Frequently I have observed the truth of this parable; when we will to forgive another person, blessings come upon them and upon ourselves. Failure to forgive causes spiritual bondage. For example, a woman married twenty years requested prayer because she had difficulty dealing with her husband's infidelity. She was understandably hurt and developed a duodenal ulcer from the stress. During the time of prayer, I asked if she were willing to forgive the husband for this betrayal, but she adamantly refused to even consider the possibility. Several weeks later I received a phone call from her daughter stating she was hospitalized with severe bleeding due to the ulcer. Visiting her in the hospital, we talked about our previous conversation and the Lord's teachings about forgiveness. "I want revenge against my husband," she sobbed, "but I realize it's going to kill me first. I can't go on this way."

Through many tears she asked Jesus to give her the strength to be willing to forgive the man who had caused so much grief in her life. We then asked the Lord to touch her physical condition and heal the ulcerative area. She looked like a different woman when I saw her several weeks later in the grocery store. The symptoms of the ulcer had nearly disappeared but she was even more excited to tell me she and her husband were seeing a marriage counselor and there was hope for reconciliation. Her willingness to forgive opened the door for the Father to bring new life into the entire situation.

Learning to walk in the Father's love and trusting him to care for our needs means daily examining our hearts to see if we are harboring grudges, hurt feelings, or desire for revenge.

*

"God, examine me and know my heart, probe me and know my thoughts" (Ps 139). Illumine my inner being with the light of your Holy Spirit to reveal any lack of forgiveness in the past or the present. Lord, help me to be willing to forgive others no matter how deeply I was wounded by rejection, insensitivity, gossip, or cruelty. Let me recall your words from the cross, "Father forgive them, they do not know what they are doing," and echo them in my own life. Please increase my awareness of the times when hurt feelings and resentments enter my heart so I may not allow bitterness to develop. To the best of my ability, enable me to forgive others so you can always deal with me in the same way—"if you forgive others their failings, your heavenly Father will forgive you yours." Thank you for all the times you have blessed me with the cleansing waters of your forgiveness.

NINE

Faith Means Peace

*I have said these things to you while still with you; but the
Advocate, the Holy Spirit whom the Father will send in my
name, will teach you everything and remind you of all I have
said to you. Peace I bequeath to you, my own peace I give to you, a
peace the world cannot give, this is my gift to you.* (Jn 14:25-27)

THE FAMILIAR SCRIPTURAL NARRATIVE describing Jesus' visit to
the home of Mary and Martha is often quoted as a reminder to
avoid the distractions of too much busyness. "Martha,
Martha, you worry and fret about so many things, and yet few
are needed..." (Lk 10:41) is an admonition which could easily
apply to the lives of most Americans. Stress, anxiety, and
tension are words frequently used to describe the prevalent
atmosphere of today's society as we constantly worry about
our health, finances, and relationships. Seminars and books on
stress management are a multi-million dollar enterprise and
tranquilizers top the list of best-selling prescription medi-
cation. Learning to control anxiety is becoming a national
pastime.

Being a follower of Jesus Christ does not automatically
confer immunity against stress because the habit patterns of
worry are firmly ingrained in our thinking. Most Christians
find it necessary to constantly discipline their thoughts in
order to avoid the pitfalls created by anxiety-producing

situations. An ancient Chinese proverb accurately describes this process: "You cannot keep the birds of worry from flying overhead, but you can stop them from making a nest in your hair." Tension is constantly present in the world around us, but we can keep it from adversely affecting our lives through the development of trust in divine providence.

Jesus exhorted the disciples to stop worrying about what they were going to eat or wear because "life means more than food, and the body more than clothing" (Lk 12:23). He wasn't encouraging occupational passivity in obtaining the necessities for living but reminding them that anxiety produces nothing. "Can any of you, for all his worrying, add a single cubit to his span of life? If the smallest things, therefore, are outside your control, why worry about the rest?" (Lk 12:26).

Being overly concerned about our "daily bread" is a waste of time and energy and creates barriers in our faith relationship with the Father. "Set your hearts on his kingdom and these other things will be given you as well" (Lk 12:31). The cure for worry is trust in the Father's ability to care for those who love him. This attitude becomes operative by setting our hearts on his kingdom and consciously choosing to stop worrying and start believing in his providence.

Daily Scripture reading and memorizing passages which promote trust in God's mercy can be valuable tools for offsetting the tendency toward anxiety. Pondering Scriptures can create the positive outlook which keeps the "birds of worry" from nesting in our hair by reminding us of God's promises to his people.

The advice Jesus gave to Martha is another method of stress management available to Christians. "Mary . . . has chosen the better part. It is not to be taken from her" (Lk 10:42). He counseled Martha to stop worrying and fretting and to sit at his feet like her sister, Mary, and listen to him. Long before the development of biofeedback techniques, Jesus recognized that quieting our busy lives and meditatively listening to God is a valuable method of dealing with tension.

We can gain a healthier perspective on our problems by following the psalmist's injunction to "pause a while and know that I am God, exalted among the nations, exalted over the earth!" (Ps 46:10). For most of us, finding time in our busy schedules to listen to the Lord involves major changes in daily routine. There are many distractions vying for attention, and we allow these to take precedence over prayer time. A nun once explained it to me very well by remarking, "Western civilization will always be poor at contemplation because we are afraid to waste time." Conditioning has taught us that productivity is a sign of success. Therefore we must do things in order to be acceptable.

However, Jesus taught Martha the value of being present to him through quiet listening, thereby gaining an advantage over worrying and fretting. He didn't tell her the kitchen work was unnecessary but that her attitude about it needed adjustment. Sitting at his feet enables us to see the duties and responsibilities of life through the eyes of Jesus and these burdens can become lighter in the process.

When I first began to learn the importance of a daily commitment to prayerful listening, I would try earnestly to complete all my household chores in order to spend time with Jesus. This was frustrating because there were always interruptions and the quiet time was postponed until it became almost non-existent. After rearranging my schedule to enable time in the morning before starting housework and child care, I was amazed at the amount of energy I had and the ease with which the chores were done. Prioritizing time to seek the kingdom of God within our hearts truly yields much fruit because faith in the Father is a natural result of spending time in his presence. How can we possibly learn to know him if we fail to sit at his feet and listen to him?

*

Dear Jesus, I am guilty of worrying and fretting about many things because my thoughts are full of anxieties about my loved ones, my health, my finances, my job. Your word reminds me that worrying about problems will not alter the situations and will often impede your blessings. Please help me to believe in the goodness of my heavenly Father and to trust in him to care for my needs. As I sit at your feet and quietly listen to your voice, reassure me of the Father's love and his willingness to watch over me and my loved ones. Please make me aware of the times when worries dominate my thoughts, so I may turn back to you and remember your promises. Increase my belief in divine providence as I learn to yield everything into his merciful care.

TEN

Faith Means Friendship

Do not let your love be a pretense, but sincerely prefer good to evil. Love each other as much as brothers should, and have a profound respect for each other . . . . If any of the saints are in need you must share with them; and you should make hospitality your special care. (Rom 12:9-13)

BECAUSE TRUST INVOLVES RELATING TO OTHERS, learning to trust in the Lord is not easily accomplished outside of a community of believers who are striving to grow in holiness. How can we have trust in God if we are unable to trust any of his creatures? "A man who does not love the brother that he can see cannot love God, whom he has never seen" (1 Jn 4:20).

Jesus' earthly life was marked by closeness and intimacy with friends. He often visited the house of Lazarus where he spent time with Mary and Martha. He seemed at ease with women which sometimes surprised his followers. He was openly criticized for his friendships with social outcasts like Zaccheus, the tax collector, and Mary Magdalene, the prostitute, yet he continued to foster these close relationships.

Perhaps his most noticeable friendships were with three of the disciples—Peter, James, and John. These men were singled out to accompany him at the raising of Jairus's daughter. They were permitted to see Jesus in splendor on Mount Tabor when his entire being was transformed into heavenly light. They were specifically named by Jesus to companion his hour of agony on the Mount of Olives before the soldiers found him and led him away.

Obviously, his relationship with these men was something special and meaningful to Jesus. These human friendships provided comfort, encouragement, and strength during times of heavy ministry and intercessory prayer. He was in constant communion with his heavenly Father, yet he still required the closeness of earthly companions. He didn't choose one type of intimacy over the other but effectively brought together human and divine interactions.

One bond of friendship which Jesus had was so deep that it was noticeable to all his followers. Thus, John was called the "disciple whom Jesus loved." We have no record that Jesus ever denied the depth of the closeness with his youngest apostle nor did he apologize to the other disciples for loving John so much. He recognized the need to have someone in his life who understood his heart and would stay with him through the Mount Tabor joy as well as the Calvary sufferings. Jesus wasn't afraid to share feelings with another. He was vulnerable on the human level and this enhanced his freedom to relate to the Father on the spiritual level.

Generally, by the time we make a commitment to follow the Good Shepherd who is Jesus Christ, we have experienced a great deal of disappointment and disillusionment in relating to others. As a result, we have erected thick, protective walls around our personality. But a decision to avoid closeness and intimacy on the human level also prevents such experiences on the spiritual level.

John's epistle clearly states it is impossible to love the unseen God if we refuse to love the brother or sister whom we can see. Willingness to trust God's action in our lives is often in direct proportion to the degree of trust we have in human relationships. In order to increase our ability to have faith in the Father's love, we must seek healing for any brokenness which keeps us from trust relationships.

We should be willing to admit any fear of intimacy and ask the Lord to heal the unhappy memories associated with broken relationships. We may have to find ways to forgive persons who have wounded us through insensitivity or rejection. Often the ones who have hurt us the most are fellow Christians: priests, sisters, prayer group leaders, members of our church or prayer community. We expect that a follower of Jesus Christ will practice the virtue of unconditional love, and when such is not the case, the devastation to our spirit causes us to resist forming more friendships. Coming to the Lord with a desire for wholeness allows his healing presence to touch our hearts and give us a fresh desire for new bonds of friendship.

If we have been the cause of another's pain due to our lack of love, we should do all that is possible to offer reconciliation. Forgiveness and continued unity are marks of Christian behavior and we have no right to withhold the kiss of peace from any brother or sister. If our offering goes unreceived we can rest in the assurance that we have done what is right and leave it in the hands of the Father.

Jesus told us that he would no longer call us servants, but friends (Jn 15:15). We welcome him into deeper union with us when we learn to accept the love of others.

*

Brother Jesus, I thank you for your example of friendship with the disciples which shows me the importance of close relationships with others. Please heal any memories of friendships which have brought sorrow and caused me to build defensive walls around myself. Lord, enable me to forgive those who rejected, criticized, or misunderstood me. Let me not hold on to these hurts from the past, but grant me the grace to accept your healing touch. Give me the courage to admit my own failures in relating to others and to apologize for my shortcomings whenever I do not behave in loving ways. May your perfect love remove fear of intimacy from my heart and help me to trust the Father's love as I learn to trust in human friendships. Enable me to develop close relationships, without expecting perfection from others. Make me willing to share my imperfections so you can make up for my deficits. Thank you for being a friend. Teach me how to befriend others.

ELEVEN

Faith Means Praise

I will bless Yahweh at all times,
his praise shall be on my lips continually;
my soul glories in Yahweh,
let the humble hear and rejoice.
Proclaim with me the greatness of Yahweh,
together let us extol his name. (Ps 34:1-3)

FAITH IN GOD CAN BE STIMULATED through exercising hymns of praise as we "make a joyful noise unto the Lord." Singing anointed hymns, reading psalms of praise, and glorifying the Lord through the charismatic gift of tongues can dispel oppression, overcome sadness, and banish the evil one who hates the sound of Christians praising their creator. As the burdens lift from our spirit, we begin to sense God's presence and his infinite love for us. Often we fail to recognize the power of praise and thus allow darkness to permeate our minds and hearts, but the Scriptures instruct us to overcome sadness with joy. The prophet Isaiah writes, "to comfort all those who mourn and to give them for ashes a garland, for mourning robe the oil of gladness, for despondency praise" (Is 61:3).

Our loving Father provides us with a recipe for despair—he will replace our mourning with the oil of gladness when we praise him. He will take away our heaviness of spirit when we come before him in openness and abandonment even when we don't feel like praising him.

Learning to glorify the name of the Lord in the midst of trials is an important step in developing a faith relationship because it demonstrates an active response to his presence. It's easy to sing praises to the Father when all is going well, but it requires death to self to put aside feelings of despair, self-pity, and depression in order to worship him.

The book of Hebrews exhorts us to "offer God an unending sacrifice of praise, a verbal sacrifice that is offered every time we acknowledge his name" (Heb 13:15). The term "sacrifice of praise" indicates that praises to the Lord might not always be ecstatic because we don't always feel like rejoicing. Sometimes we may have to admit, "Lord, I offer you the sacrifice of praise because I don't feel like praising you right now," thus sacrificing our misery by adoring him in spite of our pain. It is a sacrifice to praise when we don't feel in the mood to do so, but this type of sacrifice is very pleasing to the Lord and brings many blessings. It is a form of penance which denies our human desires in favor of the Father's will.

This attitude of heart teaches us to believe that God is truly present no matter how unhappy we feel. By introducing praise into our pain, we permit the Father to release bondages of sorrow by giving hope in the midst of trials. We demonstrate faith in God by refusing to stay stuck in self-pity.

I make a practice of listening to praise music while driving the car, cleaning my house, preparing meals, and any other appropriate time. This enables my spirit to "bless Yahweh at all times" and to have "his praise on my lips continually" (Ps 34), even when I don't feel like praising him. We are fortunate to have so much beautiful, anointed Christian music available on the radio and cassette tapes. This can be a valuable aid for keeping the power of praise moving through our spirit and into the world around us.

Often I prescribe praise music for persons who have

difficulty experiencing the presence of Jesus in their daily lives. We are sometimes oblivious to his loving care because our eyes are focused on self instead of the Father. Praise displaces the self and puts God back on the throne of our inner being where he rightfully belongs.

Recently a woman came to the house of prayer in Clearwater, Florida, where I am a staff member. She requested ministry for herself and family, giving a long history of problems with children, an alcoholic husband, her job, the neighbors—everything in her life was filled with gloom. I prayed with her but realized the task was monumental and she had to change her habit pattern of negativity.

On my advice, she purchased several tapes of praise music, promising to listen one hour each morning as she prepared for work. She returned several months later looking ten years younger and definitely happier. The problems at home hadn't changed but she discovered the recipe for happiness in the midst of pain. Thus with the psalmist she was able to say, "You have turned my mourning into dancing, you have stripped off my sackcloth and wrapped me in gladness; and now my heart, silent no longer, will play you music; Yahweh, my God, I will praise you for ever" (Ps 30:11-12).

*

Father, we do well always and everywhere to give you thanks. Help me to be willing to put aside unhappiness and enter into your courts with rejoicing. Even when I don't feel like glorifying you, give me the grace to sing a sacrifice of praise to bless you in the midst of my sorrow, pain, or loneliness. Teach me how to obtain the oil of gladness when my heart is heavy and my burdens seem overwhelming. You promised happiness to all who trust in you. Grant me the ability to have faith that you are with me even when everything appears dark and empty. I want to praise you in every moment of my life by trusting in your merciful love as I bless you at all times, your praise ever on my lips.

TWELVE

Faith Means Holiness

Since everything is coming to an end like this, you should be living holy and saintly lives while you wait and long for the Day of God to come. (2 Pt 3:11)

WHAT DOES IT MEAN TO BE HOLY? Does it imply perfection, wholeness, and sinlessness? The Scriptures say we are always to want "holiness without which no one can ever see the Lord" (Heb 12:14). Holiness gives us the ability to communicate with the Father and to have faith in his love for all of creation because holiness means to put aside anything which hinders our relationship with him. Peter advises in his letter to the early church, "Be holy in all you do, since it is the Holy One who has called you and Scripture says: 'Be holy, for I am holy'" (1 Pt 1:14).

Holiness allows the presence of Jesus to shine through us so we glow with an incandescent light. Last year I had the privilege of being at an audience of Pope John Paul II in the Vatican. As he moved throughout the assembled crowd, shaking hands and speaking to each person, I was struck by the appearance of a brightly visible light surrounding him wherever he went. I thought to myself, "No wonder we call him the Holy Father; he does appear to exude holiness."

Undoubtedly this comes from a conscious desire of John

Paul's to live in the Lord's presence every moment of his life and to do whatever is necessary to insure constant communion with the Father.

I now understand why artists throughout the centuries always paint halos around Jesus, Mary, and the saints. This is not an artistic touch but a visible reality because the light of the world is truly manifested in the followers of Jesus Christ.

Holiness doesn't mean we are perfect, but we allow the perfection of God to dwell within our hearts so it may illumine the space around us. We admit our sinful nature at each celebration of liturgy when, during the penitential rite we recite, "Lord, we have sinned against you," but we move from that position into joyfully rejoicing, "glory to God in the highest . . . ." To stay in contrition and penitence does not bring happiness to God or to ourselves because it means we lack redemption from sin. We first acknowledge our broken, human nature, but just as importantly, we must then accept the sacrifice made for us by the crucifixion and resurrection of Jesus which delivers us from all unrighteousness.

In his letter to the Romans, Paul cries out, "I know of nothing good living in me . . . instead of doing the good things I want to do, I carry out the sinful things I do not want. . . . What a wretched man I am!" (Rom 7:18-24). But Paul doesn't remain trapped in despair but goes on to acclaim, "Thanks be to God through Jesus Christ our Lord! . . . Those who are in Jesus are not condemned . . . the law of the spirit of life in Christ Jesus has set you free" (Rom 7:24; 8:1).

Repentance should always lead us from darkness into light by increasing our awareness of the Father's infinite mercy which cancels all the spiritual debts we owe. Satan keeps us focused on our sinful nature by constantly reminding us of our sins, even after we have confessed and been forgiven. He is the father of lies, distorting the truth of our salvation and making us doubt the Father's accessibility. When we no longer believe in our union with God, our faith becomes very shaky and holiness leaves our lives. We don't look, act, or talk like a person redeemed by the blood of the Lamb when false guilt takes hold of our spirit.

Several years ago I was ministering to a large prayer group in a northern city and I spent several days talking about inner healing prayer. One of the leaders of the group was a very attractive woman who seemed to walk in the light of the Lord's radiant presence, and the prayer group greatly benefitted from the holiness which she brought into the meetings. I returned to this prayer group a number of months later and I encountered the same woman. She looked years older and not at all filled with God's light. Talking with her, I learned that she was under a heavy spirit of condemnation due to an incident involving some of the prayer group members, and she had been unable to get out from under the oppression. Her inability to allow the Lord's love to shine through her was influencing others, and it took several hours of prayer and discussion before she was relieved of the burden.

It is very important to discern the difference between the conviction of the Holy Spirit bringing us to repentance for true sin and the condemnation of Satan keeping us in bondage to false guilt. When God's Spirit convicts us, we are aware of specific areas of behavior which need correction. He tells us what we have done and how we can become holy through changing our attitudes and actions. Repentance means to change our sinful nature, and change brings us closer to the Lord so his holiness can shine through.

The devil's tactics are very different. He tries to bring us under condemnation through lies: "You're no good"; "No one likes you"; "God has forsaken you"; "Remember that terrible sin you committed." Such attacks are calculated to foster doubts and fears to keep the truth of God's love from illuminating our minds. Like Paul, we can turn away from such distortions by claiming the victory over sin granted to all who profess Jesus Christ as Lord. We are holy because Jesus "has become our wisdom, and our virtue, and our holiness" (1 Cor 1:30).

*

Heavenly Father, may your name be held holy, so that all followers of your Son, Jesus Christ, may become holy in him. I praise you for allowing me to share in the splendor of your radiant presence as day and night the angelic beings sing before your throne, "Holy, Holy, Holy is the Lord God, the Almighty" (Rv 4:8). Please help me to remove any obstacles to personal holiness by making me aware of sin and giving me the grace to live a life worthy of you. I want your light to shine through my every thought, word, and action, so I will glorify your name with a spirit of holiness and bring many others to you through an example of consecrated life. Thank you for the increase of faith which follows my desire for holiness.

THIRTEEN

Faith Means Scripture Study

You must keep to what you have been taught and know to be true; remember who your teachers were, and how, ever since you were a child, you have known the holy Scriptures—from these you can learn the wisdom that leads to salvation through faith in Christ Jesus. All Scripture is inspired by God and can profitably be used for teaching, for refuting error, for guiding people's lives and teaching them to be holy. (2 Tim 3:14-16)

THE BIBLE IS THE LIVING WORD OF GOD inspired through the Holy Spirit to give us knowledge of his nature. We cannot have faith in God's goodness unless we study his word and learn to understand the person we proclaim as Lord of our lives. As we study the personality of Jesus as written in the New Testament, we begin to realize what a wonderful God we serve—how merciful, kind, and forgiving he is, thus our faith becomes stronger and more active. Jesus is God's definition of himself; he and the Father are one. Reading about the Lord's inter-actions with those around him during his earthly ministry, clarifies our concepts of the Father and his relationship to us.

Jesus used Scripture to repulse the temptations of Satan during his forty days in the desert. Often during his public ministry, the Lord quoted words from the Scriptures to teach his disciples or admonish the scribes and Pharisees. Obviously he was very knowledgeable, and no learned scholar was ever able to trap him through the use of Scripture.

Jesus took his disciples aside and "starting with Moses and going through all the prophets, he explained to them the passages throughout the Scriptures that were about himself" (Lk 24:27). He wanted his followers to understand the events of his crucifixion and resurrection in the light of biblical prophecy, for all had been foretold through the inspired writings handed down through the centuries of Jewish history.

After his resurrection from the dead, Jesus appeared to two of his disciples and accompanied them on their walk toward Emmaus. They did not recognize him, until, sharing a meal together, he broke bread and handed it to them and disappeared. Then their eyes were opened in recognition of their Lord. They exclaimed to one another, "Did not our hearts burn within us as he talked to us on the road and explained the Scriptures to us?" (Lk 24:32). Jesus continues to make the word of God burn in our hearts when we invite him to walk with us as we read and study its passages.

We can invite the Holy Spirit to open our eyes to understand the Bible, especially when we encounter difficult passages, because God's Spirit was given to us to instruct us. As Jesus explained, "I have said these things to you ... but the Advocate, the Holy Spirit, whom the Father will send in my name, will teach you everything and remind you of all I have said to you" (Jn 14:26).

I once taught a Bible study for a group of junior high school students. They were instructed to say a short prayer to the Holy Spirit before reading the Bible, to ask for wisdom, knowledge, and understanding of God's word. One young girl returned the following week with this report: "I was reading the passage where Jesus said, 'you are the salt of the earth.' It didn't make sense to me so I asked the Holy Spirit to explain what it meant. The thought came to my mind, 'What does salt do when you eat it?' I said, 'It makes you thirsty,' and the voice inside me said, 'That's what a Christian is supposed to do—make others thirsty for Jesus Christ.'" I never heard that passage preached more eloquently!

Knowledge of the Bible enables us to assist those who are searching and seeking for the truth as Philip discovered when the Lord placed him in the company of an Ethiopian eunuch who desired to understand a passage from the prophet Isaiah. Starting with the text of Isaiah 53, Philip proceeded to explain the good news of Jesus to the man; his heart was touched so deeply he asked to be baptized. Philip fulfilled his request, and the man went his way rejoicing. Knowledge of the Bible increases our effectiveness in witnessing for the Lord and gives us greater confidence in our ability to open the eyes of others.

Deepening our faith in the Father's love by immersing our spirit in his living word can be of much value in spiritual development. The rules for proper moral values, family life, and community relationships are all contained within its pages. Some Christians refer to it as the manufacturer's handbook; and indeed it is!

The apostle Paul constantly quoted Scripture in his letters to the early church, and we would be well-advised to heed the advice he gave to Timothy: "All Scripture is inspired by God and can profitably be used for teaching, for refuting error, for guiding people's lives and teaching them to be holy. This is how a man who is dedicated to God becomes fully equipped and ready for any good work" (2 Tm 3:16-17).

*

Dear Father, I praise you for giving me your word in the sacred writings of the Old and New Testament. I glorify you for providing me with an easily available source of your teachings, so I can learn to know you better by studying the Bible. Please open my eyes to recognize you in the Scriptures and let my heart burn within me as I read the anointed texts. Send your Holy Spirit to teach me the truth I need to know so my faith will be increased and my inner being strengthened. Thank you for the gift of grace the Bible brings into my life. Show me how I can better serve you by knowing your word.

FOURTEEN

Faith Means Motherhood

When Israel was a child I loved him, and I called my son out of Egypt . . . . I myself taught Ephraim to walk, I took them in my arms; yet they have not understood that I was the one looking after them. I led them with reins of kindness, with leading strings of love. I was like someone who lifts an infant close against his cheek; stooping down to him I gave him his food. (Hos 11:1, 3-4)

THE IMAGE OF GOD THE FATHER as a gentle, nurturing mother is not a contradiction in terms because God's nature contains both masculinity and femininity; "God created man in the image of himself, in the image of God he created him, male and female he created them" (Gn 1:27).

The Scriptures contain many passages alluding to the feminine dimension of the Father's love, such as the often quoted verse from Isaiah, "Does a woman forget her baby at the breast, or fail to cherish the son of her womb?" (Is 49:15). The Father in heaven embodies all the virtues of tenderness, compassion, and nurturance ordinarily ascribed to womanhood because he is a God of balance and order.

Faith in God means a willingness to open our hearts to the motherly qualities of God as well as to his fatherhood, for both sides of his nature are important to our spiritual growth. One of the most important jobs of an earthly mother is to teach her children basic trust. Psychologists tell us this developmental process takes place during the first two years of a person's life, so the mother or mother substitute is almost solely responsible for instilling trust.

She does this in a variety of ways—by providing the infant's food when he is hungry, keeping him warm and dry when he is uncomfortable, holding, rocking and singing to him when he cries. All these activities tell the baby he is wanted, loved, and cherished, so he can begin to trust in the strange world into which he was born.

As he begins to grow into a toddler, he starts to test the reality of his surroundings, but always with the presence of mother or a mother substitute to give him courage. I well remember each of my five children as they began this stage of development. As long as I was in the room, they would dare to face all kinds of dangers—climbing on the furniture, reaching for high objects, or even touching the dog. If I left the room, they would immediately begin crying. Their courage was renewed only when I returned and comforted them.

Children learn basic trust through the consistency and constancy of the mother's love, care, and vigilance for their safety. It is very difficult to trust in others or to trust in God if we have not received such treatment in the formative stages of development. However, the opportunity to grow in trust levels remains available to us through the power of prayer as we invite the Lord to give us the healing necessary to bring about deeper faith.

I believe Jesus was providing this type of help for us when from the cross he said to John, the beloved disciple, "Behold your mother." He gave this precious woman to John and to all his followers because he recognized her as the only woman who could give a mother's perfect love. Jesus knew we would all need to learn more about trusting in the Father. And Mary, his mother, is a rich resource for teaching us this trust.

She remained on earth after the Lord ascended into heaven, and helped the apostles and disciples to remain faithful to the new covenant. She stayed with them in the upper room during the long days before the Holy Spirit was poured out upon them and new life conferred.

Mary continues to bring needed graces as we invite her to pray that we experience deeper trust in divine providence. Whenever we lack faith, the mother of Jesus inspires us through her example of trust in God and her willingness to assist all who call upon her prayers.

I went through a period in my Christian journey when Mary was not a part of my spiritual life. Believing that it was a form of idolatry to seek her intercessions, I threw away my rosaries, pictures, and statues. I wanted to concentrate on Jesus and his word with no distractions. During a particularly stormy episode in my life, the Lord seemed to be very distant and unavailable. The more I sought him, the more desolate I became. At one point in the midst of the inner darkness, the Lord asked me why I was ignoring his mother. "Lord," I answered, "I want to stay close to you, not your mother." He then said to me, "Barbara, you don't honor me by avoiding my mother, for she is very dear to me. I chose her from all creation to be the human closest to my heart, and she can be a source of much comfort to you in times of distress." So I began to ask her to pray with and for me, that the Lord would be more apparent in my life. Within a few days the darkness lifted, and I was given a fresh anointing of the Holy Spirit with new gifts of healing to share with others. Mary always leads us closer to her Son, not away from him. David DuPlessis, a Pentecostal minister, has stated in an international charismatic conference, "We cannot ignore Mary in God's plan for salvation." In 1983, the Southern Baptist Conference of the United States and the American Lutheran Church at a theological seminar in Chicago signed an agreement of dialogue to study whether something of the dynamism and reality of Jesus Christ has been lost due to the elimination of Mary in their theological framework.

The woman given to us on Calvary stands firmly united with

all the people of God against the powers of evil on this earth. Many times I have been in spiritual battles for the soul of a person and have seen conversion happen through her intercession. Once at the bedside of a dying man, I prayed in every way I knew to help him accept Jesus as Lord and Savior. He had been an atheist all his life and steadfastly refused to receive Jesus Christ. As he began to lapse into a coma, I said a "Hail Mary," and as I finished the prayer, "pray for us sinners now and at the hour of our death," he opened his eyes and began to cry. He told me how miserable his life had been and how lonely he always felt. Then he asked to see a minister. It didn't take me very long to locate the hospital chaplain; the man made his peace with God and quietly died. The warfare for men's souls is very great at the time of death, and I believe Mary's prayers helped to hold back the devil's influence until salvation was secured.

Walking by faith brings continual cleansing of those parts of our being which still do not trust in the Father's love for us. Through his crucifixion, Jesus liberates us from all that prevents our faith's development. Sometimes childhood traumas make it difficult to trust in God. Often we have repressed our bad memories so that they can no longer be recognized. But if we are open and yielded to God's healing love, we can begin to comprehend the importance of the prophet's message: "When Israel was a child I loved him, and I called my son out of Egypt ... I myself taught Ephraim to walk, I took them in my arms . . . . I was like someone who lifts an infant close against his cheek; stooping down to him I gave him his food" (Hos 11:1-4).

*

Dearest Jesus, thank you for granting me the gift of your mother, Mary, so I need not lack the kind of loving care which teaches me to trust. Please heal any early childhood experiences which make it difficult for me to trust in the Father's love and mercy. Touch the early stages of my earthly life and remove any feelings of neglect, rejection, or separation. I invite you to bring your mother to fill any empty places in my heart with the warmth and tenderness of her maternal nature. May I learn to have more faith in the heavenly Father as my spirit becomes open and vulnerable to being loved and cherished. I praise you for all the ways you give me new life here on earth and prepare me for eternal life yet to come through Jesus Christ, our Lord.

FIFTEEN

Faith Means Remembering

I have tried to awaken a true understanding in you by giving you a reminder: recalling to you what was said in the past by the holy prophets and the commandments of the Lord and Savior which you were given by the apostles. We must be careful to remember that during the last days there are bound to be people who will be scornful . . . and ask, "Well, where is this coming?" (2 Pt 3:2-4)

OUR FAITH RELATIONSHIP WITH THE FATHER sometimes goes through episodes of dryness and desolation. It may appear as if God has abandoned us because we feel so devoid of his presence. At such times we may begin to question whether or not we have faith, or we may even doubt the existence of God.

Recognizing that such an experience is normal can lessen some of our fears. Reading the lives of the saints, we find ample evidence that the spiritual journey contains numerous occasions of emptiness and doubt.

Pope John XXIII wrote a diary, published under the title *Journal of a Soul,* containing reflections of his life from the seminary to the papacy and detailing many interior struggles to trust in divine providence. The road to sanctification doesn't guarantee the absence of doubt, but provides numerous opportunities to deepen our faith relationship with God by walking through spiritual deserts.

Each of us could benefit from Pope John's example by keeping a spiritual journal of our faith relationship with the Father. Along with his descriptions of desolation, Pope John also wrote about the moments of joy, consolation, and peace—memories which undoubtedly sustained him throughout the responsibilities of his priesthood. Time has a way of dulling our memory, causing us to forget moments of glory and joy when union with God seemed real and tangible. Writing a history of such experiences enables us to remember the favors granted by the Lord and promotes gratitude for his kindnesses toward us.

Daily prayer time should begin with thanksgiving; keeping a personal diary helps us to recall God's infinite mercy during the times he poured out his Spirit upon us. Remembrances of past blessings encourage us to trust the Father's continuing care. As the psalmist wrote, "I thank you, Yahweh, with all my heart, because you have heard what I said. . . . I give thanks to your name for your love and faithfulness; your promise is even greater than your fame. The day I called for help, you heard me and you increased my strength" (Ps 138:1-3).

Our spiritual diary should include a record of times of unhappiness and seemingly unanswered prayer along with the victorious occasions because we often learn more from the former than the latter. God's apparent absences can be instructive when we ask him to reveal how our spiritual life has benefitted from this turn of events. "How has this dryness caused me to draw closer to you? What have I learned from this experience of desolation?" Such reflections can deepen our faith in God by concentrating our thoughts on the positive rather than the negative.

Keeping a spiritual diary helps us to see patterns of consolation and desolation and to understand our spiritual growth and development. We can remember the moments of joy and praise the Father's infinite mercy; we can recall the times of sadness and rejoice in his ability to teach through suffering. Thus nothing is wasted in our journey of faith.

Each time I look over my personal writings of day to day life in the Spirit, I'm always amazed at the ways the Lord has been leading me to trust him more and more. Times of heaviness always precede experiences of new life and there are always warnings of impending difficulties when I listen to his voice in my quiet time.

Recording my walk with the Lord gives fresh insights into his personality because it focuses my thoughts on the important aspects of this relationship and clarifies my perspective. My relationship with Jesus becomes more and more real with each page of remembrances. It becomes almost a love letter between myself and the Lord that I can read over in quiet contemplation.

Perhaps the prophet Habakkuk had something similar in mind when he told the Hebrews to, "Write the vision down, inscribe it on tablets to be easily read" (Hb 2:2). Heeding his advice will help us grow in faith as we remember the Lord's faithful care and concern. Then we can thank the Lord in all our ways.

*

Heavenly Father, I praise you for the many times you have blessed my life with good gifts of joy, love, and peace. I remember moments of union with you which brought deep consolation to my spirit, mind, and body. Thank you for the tenderness and compassion you have shown to me. Grant me the ability to perceive your presence even in times of emptiness and dryness as I try to see these experiences through your eyes and understand them with your heart. Help me to recognize divine mercy in every circumstance of my life, for you have promised to rescue, protect, and deliver all who call upon your name. As I ponder all these things in moments of quiet reflection, may my trust increase through remembering and may I always keep in my heart the truth of your love.

SIXTEEN

Faith Means Warfare

Nothing therefore can come between us and the love of Christ, even if we are troubled or worried, or being persecuted, or lacking food or clothes or being threatened or even attacked. . . . These are the trials through which we triumph, by the power of him who loved us. (Rom 8:35-37)

THERE ARE TWO KINGDOMS in the world of the spirit—one belongs to God, the other to Satan. Many do not believe that Satan exists; even ministers of the gospel sometimes teach that man creates his own evil and is solely responsible for all the world's darkness. But Jesus gives a very different picture when he tells his disciples, "I watched Satan fall like lightning from heaven. Yes, I have given you power to tread underfoot serpents and scorpions and the whole strength of the enemy; nothing shall ever hurt you" (Lk 10:18-19).

The Lord doesn't deny the existence of Satan, but reminds us of the way this mighty angel, Lucifer, lost his position in the Father's kingdom. The book of Revelation tells how a great war broke out in heaven when Michael with his angels attacked the dragon, "the primeval serpent, known as the devil or Satan, who had deceived all the whole world, was hurled down to earth and his angels were hurled down with him" (Rv 12:7-19). The word of God warns us that trouble is coming to the earth "because the devil has gone down to you in a rage, knowing that his days are numbered" (Rv 12:12).

The devil spoken about in the Scriptures is a real entity, not a mythical character dressed in a red suit with pointed horns and a long tail. He possesses two characteristics which cause problems for Christians who are desiring to live by faith in the Lord: he is a liar and a deceiver. His favorite ploy is to make us doubt his existence, so we fail to protect against his attacks. Jesus confirms the reality of Satan but reminds his followers he has given us power to "tread underfoot the whole strength of the enemy." The world of darkness cannot defeat us when we utilize the power of the blood of Jesus Christ.

Faith in God gives us the assurance that the battle is over even though spiritual warfare continues. "He has overridden the Law, and cancelled every record of the debt that we had to pay; he has done away with it by nailing it to the cross; and so he got rid of the Sovereignties and the Powers, and paraded them in public, behind him in his triumphal procession" (Col 2:14). Whenever the Roman legions returned from a successful battle, they marched into Rome with the defeated enemy walking behind as a sign of their servitude to the empire. In the spiritual world, Jesus has already done this to show the world he is King.

Satan lies and tries to convince us that God is not with us, that we are not saved by the blood of the Lamb, that the Lord isn't interested in our problems. He attempts to coerce believers into doubting the Father's ability to bring peace, justice, and healing. He constantly reminds us of the sin in our lives so that we will feel unclean and guilt-ridden. Distortion of the truth is the name of his game, and recognizing these tactics is an important part of our growth in trusting God.

Knowing the promises given to us in the Scriptures is an excellent method of combating Satan's deceits. Jesus employed the word of God during his time of prayer and fasting in the wilderness to turn away the devil's temptations. It is helpful to memorize several uplifting Bible quotations for times of spiritual oppression or depression. My favorite is from Romans: "For I am certain of this: neither death nor life, no angel, no prince, nothing that exists, nothing still to come, not any power, or height or depth, nor any created thing, can ever come between us and the love of God made visible in Christ Jesus our Lord" (Rom 8:38-39). This passage has sustained me during times of great turmoil when I could not sense the Father's presence in any way except by faith in his word. Satan will try every trick to make us doubt God's love, but we have a wealth of armaments available in the living word of God.

For a number of years the Catholic Church practiced the recitation of the prayer to St. Michael the Archangel at the end of every mass. This prayer, given to Pope Leo XIII on October 13, 1884, was prompted by a conversation he heard between the devil and Jesus in which the evil one boasted that he could destroy the Lord's church if he had more power and more time. Jesus is reported to answer his request with the stipulation that Satan could have only one hundred more years to accomplish the destruction of the church. Pope Leo was given to understand that the people of God would also be given more power to repulse the attacks of the enemy, and he composed the prayer to St. Michael as a means of appropriating such strength from the heavenly army.

I have personally found this prayer to be extremely efficacious in times of trial, and we make a practice of saying it daily at Our Lady of Divine Providence House of Prayer. As we learn to trust in the Father, we should expect to encounter resistance from the evil one, but forewarned is forearmed. Recognizing the adversary and putting on the full armor of Jesus Christ gives us the spiritual power to "tread on all the strength of the enemy." The letter of Peter tells us to "Be calm but vigilant . . . . Stand up to him, *strong in faith*" (1 Pt 5:9-10).

*

Almighty Father, I praise you for giving me the victory over Satan through the death and resurrection of your Son,

Jesus Christ. I confidently stand firm and trust you as I call upon Michael and his angels to fight the spiritual battle for me and for my loved ones.

"St. Michael the Archangel, defend us in the battle; be our protection against the malice and snares of the devil. May God restrain him, we humbly pray, and do thou, O prince of the heavenly host, by the Divine power cast into hell Satan and all the other evil spirits who roam through the world seeking the ruin of souls."

(Copies of the full prayer can be obtained from: Apostolate of Christian Action, P.O. Box 24, Fresno, CA 93707.)

SEVENTEEN

Faith Means Hope

And indeed everything that was written long ago in the Scripture was meant to teach us something about hope from the examples Scripture gives of how people who did not give up were helped by God . . . . May the God of hope bring you such joy and peace in your faith that the power of the Holy Spirit will remove all bounds to hope. (Rom 15:4, 35)

THE DICTIONARY DEFINES the word "hope" as a verb meaning "to look forward with confidence of fulfillment; to expect with desire." Like the word "faith," hope is an action word which energizes us with trust in the Father's mercy and love. It causes anticipation of future events with a sense of confidence in better things to come because we believe God is creating a "new heaven and a new earth" even when there is little evidence to confirm such belief.

Paul wrote a letter to the Romans which clearly states the Christian view of life: "The whole creation is eagerly waiting for God to reveal his sons. . . . creation still retains the hope of being freed, like us, from its slavery to decadence, to enjoy the same freedom and glory as the children of God" (Rom 8:19-22). The J.B. Phillips translation of the Bible gives this passage an interesting flavor: "The whole creation is on tiptoe to see the wonderful sight of the sons of God coming into their own."

It's fun to imagine trees, shrubs, and flowers waiting with joyful anticipation the return of Jesus Christ and the establishment of his kingdom. Glenn Clark wrote an interesting little book called *The Man Who Talks With the Flowers* in which he tells that George Washington Carver's conversations with the flowers gave him the secrets which revolutionized the agriculture of the Southern United States. Creation does indeed retain the hope of seeing the earth transformed into newness of life.

Faith in God puts us in an attitude of hope which transcends all the pain and suffering of the world. Hope enables us to continue on the journey of faith in spite of set-backs, obstacles, and resistances. "For we must be content to hope that we shall be saved—our salvation is not in sight, we should not have to be hoping for it if it were—but, as I say . . . it is something we must wait for with patience" (Rom 8:24-25).

Patience while waiting for God to fulfill his promises is one of the marks of a hope-filled heart. The Israelites retained such hope throughout centuries of persecutions and slavery because they constantly reminded one another of Yahweh's promise of deliverance. Whenever they began to falter, the Father sent prophets to repeat his words once again, so they would not lose heart.

Elizabeth commended her cousin, Mary, with the words, "Blessed is she who believed that the promise made her by the Lord would be fulfilled" (Lk 1:45). Mary had not yet seen the completion of the message given to her by the angel Gabriel, but she believed, hoped, trusted, and lived as one who knew the Father always honored his word. She experienced more than thirty years of exile, misunderstanding, and sorrow before the angel's prophecy was manifested through Jesus, her son. She had moments of anxiety, such as when the young Jesus was lost in Jerusalem for three days: "See how worried your father and I have been, looking for you" (Lk 2:48). Yet, on Calvary, she held firmly to her trust in God by her actions—

"Near the cross stood his mother" (Jn 19:25). Even in the agony of the death of her son, Mary remained hopeful, knowing in her heart it would reflect the glory of God.

Often in our personal spiritual journey, the Lord gives us insights about future developments, and we become excited over these prospects. Frequently such revelations are followed by a long period of dryness, frustration, or emptiness which causes us to question whether or not we heard the Lord correctly. During such times it is helpful to remember St. Paul's counsel: "it is something we must wait for with patience." God's timing is very different from ours; therefore, hope is essential to the development of our faith because it builds confidence as we wait for the revelation to be brought forth.

When the Lord called me into a public speaking and healing ministry, he spoke the following words which I wrote in my spiritual diary, August 15, 1969. "Take heart in the experiences of your week as a speaker in the West Virginia Camp Farthest Out; it is but the beginning of a long and glorious ministry in my service. You need not fear what is to come, but put yourself into my loving arms; I'll never let you down." At that time the Lord showed me that we would be moving from Illinois and many doors would open for the healing ministry. We did not move for six years, and the fulfillment of this word only began to be born with the opening of the House of Prayer here in Clearwater, Florida, in 1980. During those years I had many occasions to wonder if I had misunderstood the message given to me, but I continued to walk with the light he gave me each day.

In retrospect, I see the wisdom of the Lord, for I had much to learn about walking by faith. He only delays in answering our prayers and completing his promises because there is good reason for the waiting period. Each challenge to faith is a rich opportunity to practice hope by patiently waiting upon his perfect timing.

*

Gentle Father, I pray for the gift of hope to sustain my faith in you and in your promises to me. Enable me to be confident in expecting you to bless me and my loved ones with the good gifts which ensure salvation. Grant me patience as I wait for your kingdom to come. Help me to keep my eyes on you, ever trusting in your desire to bring healing and peace into my life. Thank you for the gift of hope which lifts my spirit to praise your holiness and splendor. Through the sacrifice of your Son, Jesus Christ, I place my hope in you.

EIGHTEEN

Faith Means Discipline

Yet, since you love sincerity of heart,
teach me the secrets of wisdom.
Purify me with hyssop until I am clean;
wash me until I am whiter than snow.

Instill some joy and gladness into me,
let the bones you have crushed rejoice again.
Hide your face from my sins,
wipe out all my guilt.

God, create a clean heart in me,
put into me a new and constant spirit,
do not banish me from your presence,
do not deprive me of your Holy Spirit. (Ps 51:6-11)

OUR FAITH IN GOD CAN GROW when we discipline our minds away from the impurity, violence, and occultism of today's society and toward the holiness and virtue of God's kingdom. Anything which distracts us from the Lord can keep us from trusting in him. We cannot put faith in God and at the same time practice the world's values, for darkness and light cannot inhabit the same space.

The Scriptures tell us to fill our minds "with everything that is true, everything that is noble, everything that is good and pure, everything that we love and honor, and everything that can be thought virtuous or worthy of praise.... Then the God of peace will be with you" (Phil 4:8-9). It is very difficult to establish a meaningful relationship with the Father when the mind is occupied with unhealthy thoughts. The media is constantly bombarding us with impure images and sensuous messages. The world of advertising is given over to selling products through sexually stimulating commercials and bill-boards. We cannot totally avoid this psychological invasion of our minds, but we can keep from dwelling on the sensuality it provokes or from deliberately watching or reading immoral material.

We often excuse this behavior by rationalizing that it doesn't hurt anyone when we watch suggestive movie scenes or read erotic books and magazines, but we fail to recognize the damage it does to our own personhood. If we fill the beautiful mind given to us by God with impurity, it attaches itself to our spirit, and the light of Jesus becomes darkened in our heart. We cannot divide up the various components of our being; the body, mind, and spirit are interrelated in such a way that whatever happens in one part of us is going to affect the rest. Physicians are well aware of the wear and tear of the mind on the body in the form of psychosomatic symptoms.

Usually the erosion of our spirit happens very slowly. We are unaware of the subtle way faith is being undermined by our bad habits. Being addicted to the afternoon "soaps" or habitually reading romance novels may seem a rather tame form of activity in comparison to all the many more violent types of behavior, but these stories always portray infidelity, dishonesty, and seduction in ways that seem normal and natural.

The Bible exhorts us to fill our minds with everything good and pure so the peace of God can be in us. We can choose not to fill our minds with any impurities and thus provide space in our minds for God's goodness and holiness to develop. This will do much to nurture the mustard seed of faith in the Lord because it communicates life to our spirit.

I recall praying with a man who wanted to experience more of the Lord's presence in his life. Many months of knocking, seeking, and asking did not seem to be producing inner peace and he was becoming despondent. Finally he revealed his addiction to pornographic films and asked me to pray for a release from this control in his life. His willingness to abandon this behavior opened the door for the Lord to begin blessing him and his family. As long as he permitted his mind to be filled with darkness, the light of Christ could not penetrate his spirit. His faith in God was activated when he surrendered his will into the will of the Father.

A not-so-subtle form of darkness can militate against our faith in God when we entertain occult practices, such as ouija boards, tarot cards, palm reading, horoscopes, seances, fortune telling, yoga, automatic writing, and so on. Even if we don't really believe in evil spirits, our spirit is adversely affected when we seek answers from sources outside of God's Holy Spirit. Renouncing such practices and asking Jesus Christ to cover the doorpost of our mind with his precious blood, can enable us to concentrate on those things which bring faith, hope, and love. If our involvement in the occult has been more than just a passing acquaintance, we may need to seek the help of a priest, minister, or prayer group to be released from the spiritual bondage. Above all, we must always maintain the proper perspective; "you have in you one who is greater than anyone in this world" (1 Jn 4:4). There is no need to be fearful of Satan's power when we walk in the light of the Lord. Jesus prayed for us, "I am not asking you to remove them from the world, but to protect them from the evil one" (Jn 17:15). We can accept the grace from this prayer by cooperating with the Holy Spirit and disciplining ourselves in every way necessary. By so doing, we bring greater faith in God's love into every aspect of our lives.

*

Loving Father, I ask you to forgive me for allowing my mind to dwell on things which are not edifying and life-giving. I want to fill my mind with everything that is true, pure, noble, good, and worthy of praise, so your Spirit can live in each part of my being. I renounce all superstitious or occult practices and ask you to cleanse my mind and heart from such defilement. I willingly put my trust in you through your Son, Jesus Christ, and no longer put faith in the powers of darkness. I promise to bring more discipline into my thoughts so the immorality of the world cannot find a home in me. Thank you for giving me the courage to remain true to you and your love for me.

NINETEEN

Faith Means Adoration

Come, bless Yahweh,
all you who serve Yahweh,
Serving in the house of Yahweh,

in the courts of the house of our God!
Stretch out your hands towards the sanctuary,
bless Yahweh night after night!

May Yahweh bless you from Zion,
he who made heaven and earth! (Ps 134:1-3)

MOTHER ANGELICA, the Abbess of a cloistered monastery in Birmingham, Alabama, is a woman of great faith. Her ability to trust God resulted in the construction, on the ground of the monastery, of the world's first Roman Catholic cable television network. A huge satellite dish behind the convent beams hundreds of hours of Christian programming into homes throughout the United States on the Eternal Word Television Network.

Mother and her fifteen sisters also print thousands of booklets, tracts, and pamphlets which they ship throughout the world for purposes of evangelization. How does this Poor Clare nun with no prior knowledge of printing, publishing, or telecasting receive the faith to undertake such massive projects for furthering God's kingdom on earth?

She has great devotion to the eucharistic presence of Jesus Christ and established Our Lady of the Angels Monastery with a chapel of perpetual adoration where, enthroned above the altar, is the body of Jesus Christ which is constantly adored by Mother and the sisters. Besides their many duties, each of them spends two or three hours a day in contemplative prayer before the real presence of Jesus in the sacred host. Mother Angelica believes that her faith in God has grown in direct proportion to the amount of time she spends in adoration of her Lord.

Bishop Fulton Sheen, whose TV teachings touched millions of viewers, discovered the same truth about adoration of the Lord. He also prioritized two hours of prayer time every day in the presence of Jesus in the Blessed Sacrament and cited this practice as the source of power behind all his priestly endeavors. He encouraged all Christians to recognize the tremendous gift of graces to be obtained from this devotional practice.

Sr. Breige McKenna, a Catholic nun anointed with a worldwide healing ministry, insists that all speaking engagements must allow two hours for her daily eucharistic worship. She believes this discipline increases her faith, undergirds her gift of healing, and allows many miracles to occur.

Mother Teresa of India, another advocate of adoration, teaches her sisters to pray before the Blessed Sacrament for an hour each morning. Occasionally she is criticized for this practice by people who remind her that thousands of sick and dying outside of her door need attention while the sisters waste time in prayer. Mother Teresa gently explains, "We have nothing to share with the poor and dying unless we allow Jesus Christ to fill us with the richness of his Spirit as we sit in his presence." She understands that those who are poor in spirit are truly the most deprived. Daily quiet time before the Blessed Sacrament brings Mother and her sisters an inner wealth which communicates life to their apostolate.

Several years ago we instituted eucharistic adoration on Wednesdays at Our Lady of Divine Providence House of Prayer in Clearwater, Florida. We spend this day in prayer for the diocese of St. Petersburg, asking Jesus to bless the bishop, priests, sisters, brothers, lay ministers, and seminarians with spiritual renewal.

One day as I was kneeling before the monstrance containing the sacred host, the Lord spoke this question in my heart: "Barbara, what would happen this morning if Fr. Justin placed a container of radioactive uranium on the altar?" "The chapel would become radioactive," I answered. He asked me to consider the effect this would have on those sitting in the room and I imagined radioactivity entering each of us. "Would you become immediately aware this was happening?" the Lord continued. "No, the early signs of radioactive penetration are so slight that only microscopic examination would reveal the cellular changes," I thought. Reflecting on this exchange I recalled Moses' experience on Mount Sinai: "As he came down from the mountain . . . he did not know that the skin on his face was radiant after speaking with Yahweh. And when Aaron and all the sons of Israel saw Moses, the skin on his face shone so much that they would not venture near him. And when Moses finished speaking to them, he put a veil over his face" (Ex 34:29-34).

Contemplating the Lord brings about tiny changes in our body, mind, and spirit which may not be instantly obvious but which become apparent as we continue the practice. Microscopic transformations within our being can increase our faith as we allow the Father to penetrate deeply into our hearts.

Many Catholic churches have regularly scheduled times of adoration which make it possible for us to join in this important time of prayer. Also, the Lord remains present in the tabernacle every minute of the day and night, and we can sit in his presence following mass or at other times that suit our schedule. If we are unable to go to church, we can still remain in quiet reverence before his majesty in the closet of our heart. Jesus patiently waits for us to enter into his presence, for it will do much to stimulate the growth of our faith in him.

*

Heavenly Father, I ponder the mystery of Jesus' precious body, blood, soul, and divinity present in the eucharist and thank you for granting this wonderful sacrament which permits me to come close to you in such an intimate way. Please increase my trust in your care as I remain in your presence. Let me become more aware of your love for me as I am bathed in the radiance of your beautiful light. Infuse my spirit with the power of your love so that my face might shine with the same brilliance Moses knew. "And we, with our unveiled faces reflecting like mirrors the brightness of the Lord, all grow brighter and brighter as we are turned into the image that we reflect; this is the work of the Lord who is Spirit" (2 Cor 3:18).

TWENTY

Faith Means Fatherhood

"I am the Way, the Truth and the Life. No one can come to the Father except through me. If you know me, you know my Father too. From this moment you know him and have seen him. . . . To have seen me is to have seen the Father." (Jn 14:7-9)

JESUS TAUGHT US TO CALL GOD "OUR FATHER," a title having tremendous implications. The almighty one, creator of the universe, omnipotent and powerful, invites us to enter into a union so intimate that we can be called sons and daughters of the most high God. What an unbelievable gift this is! No wonder the psalmist sang:

I look up at your heavens, made by your fingers,
at the moon and stars you set in place—
ah, what is man that you should spare a thought for him,
the son of man that you should care for him? (Ps 8:3-4)

The almighty God came to earth in the person of Jesus to teach us to relate to him as Father. "To have seen me is to have seen the Father" (Jn 14:9). Looking at Jesus we behold the true personality of God.

We cannot really have faith in the Father unless we enter into a Father-son or Father-daughter relationship with him. As long as he remains some abstract entity somewhere out in space, we fail to comprehend the tenderness of his mercy or the depth of his love. It's difficult to entrust ourselves to a stranger, but Jesus shows us that God is a friend, closer to us than our human family.

Many Christians have no difficulty understanding God as a loving Father. Therefore they approach him with faith and trust in his divine goodness, believing he will care for them with paternal tenderness. St. Therese of Lisieux, known as the Little Flower, was such a person. She had no doubts about God's constant attention and brought every detail of her life to him. Calling it her "little way," she taught the sisters of her Carmelite order to trust the Father for everything. Although she never ventured from the cloistered convent and died at the young age of twenty-four, her teachings affected many people. She was one of the few saints canonized by popular acclaim within twenty-eight years of her death, and today she remains one of the best-known saints of the church and an example of a woman who had great faith because she believed in God as a loving Father.

One of the reasons for Therese's ability to so easily accept the fatherhood of God was the beautiful relationship she had with her natural father, Louis Martin. By her own admission, she was greatly spoiled and always affirmed by him; thus she was formed throughout her childhood to trust and rely on her earthly father. This attitude was then transferred toward the heavenly Father and produced a deep belief in his infinite goodness.

Persons who have not been surrounded with such a positive influence may find it very hard to open their hearts to the Father in heaven. If their earthly father is absent, abusive, unaffirming, or unable to demonstrate warmth or affection, the child learns to mistrust and erects walls of resistance to keep out anyone who might cause further pain. Occasionally the relationship with an earthly father is so traumatic that mentioning the term "father" can cause fear and anxieties to erupt.

A Catholic nun with a prison ministry told me the following story: "When I first began this apostolate, I made a practice of bringing greeting cards to the prisoners at times of special holidays so they could send them to their relatives. I couldn't supply them with enough cards for Mother's Day because the demand was very great, so I really stocked up for Father's Day. I ended up returning all the cards to the stores because the prisoners were not interested in writing to their fathers. Most of them had never known a father's love, and the mention of this relationship brought much bitterness from them."

These negative experiences cause us to project the image of a tyrannical, cold, distant, or judgmental father onto the person of God, the Father; our mind is distorted through the conditioning we've received. If our concept of father isn't healthy, then we have great difficulty permitting God to father us.

Our faith relationship with the Lord can be strengthened when we invite Jesus to heal us of the painful memories which impede our ability to accept God as a loving Father. The prophet Isaiah said Jesus would bear our sufferings and carry our sorrows, and "through his wounds we are healed" (Is 53:5). The Lord nailed to the cross everything which keeps us from the fullness of life; he transformed all our sorrows releasing us from bondage to the past.

This great sacrifice enables us to walk with Jesus into each painful life experience and to ask his healing touch to free our hearts from negative father relationships, so we can truly accept our rightful role as a son or daughter of God.

*

Dearest Jesus, you told us no one could come to the Father except through you; please help me to really know the Father's love. Heal me of any memories of my earthly father which prevent total union with God. Help me to overcome any fear of intimate relationship with God so I may truly call him my Father and accept my rightful position as a son or daughter in his kingdom. I want to experience the Father's affirming love just as Jesus did when the Lord proclaimed, "You are my Son, the Beloved; my favor rests on you" (Lk 3:22). Speak this same word of truth into my own heart that I may no longer doubt my relationship with you, for I am your beloved. I rejoice in this great gift of life forever and ever.

TWENTY-ONE

Faith Means Changes

*You have stripped off your old behavior with your old self, and
you have put on a new self which will progress toward true
knowledge the more it is renewed in the image of its creator. . . .
There is only Christ: he is everything and he is in everything.*
(Col 3:9, 11)

SOMETIMES WE FAIL TO RECEIVE the desired answers to prayer
because we refuse to comply with the conditions the Father
asks of us. A person who prays for healing of emphysema but
who continues to smoke is exercising a type of faith which
demands divine intervention without human effort. True faith
in God means a willingness to do our part so that the Father
can do his part.

The serenity prayer is a beautiful example of this principle of
faith: "God grant me the serenity to accept the things I cannot
change, the courage to change the things I can, and the
wisdom to know the difference."

This attitude of trust in God acknowledges areas in our lives
which cannot be changed because they are beyond human
power to do so. A person grieving over the loss of a loved one
must eventually accept the situation or risk becoming
emotionally and physically affected. When there is nothing
more we can do to alter a situation, we can ask the Lord to
grant us peace and serenity in the midst of it.

The second part of the serenity prayer seeks courage to "change the things we can." This indicates a willingness to cooperate with the Father by removing impediments to his graces. Refusing to change the things we can is an attitude which seeks God's help yet stubbornly wants things done our way and not his.

This attitude is illustrated in the story of the man whose home was threatened by floodwaters and a neighbor drove by in his truck to offer rescue assistance. "No thanks," he replied, "I'm trusting in the Lord to take care of me." Soon the water flowed into his home and a friend in a motor boat offered to take him to higher ground. "No thanks," he again replied; "I'm trusting in the Lord to take care of me." As the waters continued to rise, he sought refuge on the roof and a helicopter pilot begged him to come aboard. He again answered, "No thanks, I'm trusting in the Lord." The raging waters swept him away and he was drowned. As he entered the gates of heaven he said, "Lord, I put my trust in you; why didn't you save me?" And Jesus replied, "I sent you a truck, a boat, and a helicopter. What more did you want?"

The man was demanding that God answer his prayer in accordance with his own survival plan and not God's design. He wanted the Lord to do something with no human intervention or effort, and so reaped the consequences of his stubbornness.

Faith means exercising all that is within our power, thus opening the door for God's power to operate. It is presumptuous to believe in the Father's ability to bring good into our lives if we refuse to do what we can to facilitate the process. If we are not a part of the solution, then we are a part of the problem.

The Father loves us too much to treat us like mindless robots incapable of doing anything on our own. He challenges us to grow by giving us opportunities to align our will with his will.

A member of one of the aristocratic Jewish families came to Jesus with the question, "Master, what have I to do to inherit eternal life?" Jesus reminded him of the necessity of obeying the commandments given by God to Moses and the man replied, "I have kept all these from my earliest days till now." When Jesus heard this, he said, "There is still one thing you lack. Sell all that you own and distribute the money to the poor, and you will have treasure in heaven; then come, follow me." When the man heard this he was filled with sadness for he was very rich (Lk 18:18-23). His unwillingness to fulfill the conditions which would bring the eternal life he was seeking prevented Jesus from answering his request. He wanted to keep his wealth more than he desired new life, and he went away very depressed.

We exercise faith in the Father's love when we do the things he asks of us, no matter how difficult they might be. Our trust in God is activated when we are willing to courageously change the behaviors, attitudes, or habits which are barriers to the Christian life. For example, we demonstrate a desire to receive healing when we eat a proper diet, incorporate rest and recreation into our daily routine, and avoid unhealthy activities.

The third part of the serenity prayer asks for the wisdom to know when to accept a situation and when to change it. This is an important element but the discernment to know how to proceed is not easily achieved, and we often need outside counsel. When we are confronted with an area of life which causes us uncertainty, we should be willing to submit it to a prayer group leader, pastor, or trusted prayer partner who can assist us to know the will of God for us.

Learning to know the mind of God requires that we continually listen to his voice in our quiet time of personal prayer. "If there is any one of you who needs wisdom, he must ask God, who gives to all freely and ungrudgingly; it will be given to him" (Jas 1:5).

*

Dear Lord, grant me the courage to change the things I can in my life. Give me the strength to give up the bad habits or unhealthy behavior or destructive relationship which is a barrier to your graces being poured out upon me. Help me be willing to change and to cooperate with you to bring about the answers to prayer that I seek. Let me not refuse to fulfill any conditions you ask of me as I put my trust in you by willingly accepting your way and relinquishing my way. Please give me peace in those situations which cannot be changed, and the wisdom to recognize them.

TWENTY-TWO

Faith Means Sacrifice

Come to me, all you who labor and are overburdened, and I will give you rest. Shoulder my yoke and learn from me, for I am gentle and humble in heart, and you will find rest for your souls. Yes, my yoke is easy and my burden light." (Mt 11:28-30)

THE ANCIENT ISRAELITES LEARNED to have faith in Yahweh through the example of their father Abraham; "he put his faith in God, and this faith was considered as justifying him" (Gal 3:6).

When I first began to study the Scriptures, the story of Abraham and his son Isaac was a source of confusion for me. The book of Genesis reports that God put him to this test: "Take your son, your only child Isaac, whom you love, and go to the land of Moriah. There you shall offer him as a burnt offering, on a mountain I will point out to you" (Gn 22:2).

Abraham did as he was told. He collected wood, constructed an altar, bound his son Isaac, and placed him upon the wood. As he was about to kill him with a knife, an angel of the Lord intervened and told him not to raise his hand against the boy; "Do not harm him, for now I know you fear God. You have not refused me your son, your only son" (Gn 22:12).

How can we reconcile this story with the words, "God is love"? Can a loving Father require such a sacrifice? Is it possible to have a faith relationship with a deity that tests his people in this manner?

In order to understand this passage, it's important to realize that Abraham lived his entire life in a pagan world. Until his encounter with Yahweh, Abraham worshipped numerous gods and goddesses, making sacrifices to them as did everyone around him. Human sacrifices were common to ancient cultures, and it would not have seemed extraordinary for Abraham to consider offering his son to Yahweh as a form of homage. Looking at it from this perspective we can understand his willingness to be obedient in proving his submission to God by giving his most precious possession, Isaac, the son he loved.

The great revelation for Abraham was the intervention of the sacrifice—Yahweh refused this gift because he wanted the father of his chosen people to dramatically understand his relationship to God was not based on human sacrifices. Yahweh intended to pour out his blessings on Abraham and his descendants without the ritual death of men, women, and children so common in the pagan religious rites. This truth was presented so strongly that it would always be taught to those who were to become the nation of Israel. The God they were following wanted a different relationship with his people because he was not like any other god, and he clearly established that fact through the experience of Abraham and Isaac.

This enabled the psalmist to proclaim:

Sacrifice gives you no pleasure,
were I to offer holocaust, you would not have it.
My sacrifice is this broken spirit,
you will not scorn this crushed and broken heart.

(Ps 51:16-17)

The Father desires our offering of brokenness, rejection, loneliness, sorrow, and pain to be brought to his altar. He wants us to demonstrate respect for him by believing he cares about our daily struggles to earn a living or care for children or overcome temptations. He patiently waits for us to bring him broken hearts, so he might consume them with the fire of his love.

The Aztecs of Mexico ritually removed the hearts of the humans sacrificed to the serpent-god they worshipped. They believed these hearts, when thrown onto the fire, would bring blessings. Our Father in heaven asks us to yield hearts in a spiritual way—the only way which brings wholeness, peace, and life.

We fail to respond to God's desire for sacrifice when we hold on to suffering, when we clutch it to ourselves and refuse to let go. Such an attitude obstructs the Father's love and makes it difficult to receive the blessings he has for us. We must yield the Isaacs in our lives as willingly as Abraham did, trusting God to act mercifully on our behalf.

God's nature doesn't change. He is the same yesterday, today, and forever; therefore, we can give him our broken spirits and crushed hearts, confident he will not "quench the smoldering wick or crush the bruised reed" of our souls (Is 42:3).

*

Dearest Father, you desire me to demonstrate faith by sacrificing all that is dear to me just as Abraham did. Help me to place everything in my life on your altar—all my heartaches, needs, and sufferings. Let me not withhold these things from you because I fear you won't accept my offering or be concerned with my needs. Lord, I believe in your mercy as I yield myself to you; I thank you for accepting my sorrows and pain. Grant me the grace to continually sacrifice every part of my life to the God who cares.

TWENTY-THREE

Faith Means Joy

"I tell you most solemnly, you will be weeping and wailing, while the world will rejoice; you will be sorrowful, but your sorrow will turn to joy. A woman in childbirth suffers, because her time has come; but when she has given birth to the child she forgets the suffering in her joy that a man has been born into the world. So it is with you: you are sad now, but I shall see you again, and your hearts will be full of joy, and that joy no one shall take from you." (Jn 16:20-22)

"HAPPY THE MAN who puts his trust in you" (Ps 84:12). The words of this beautiful psalm tell us a person who trusts in God should experience happiness in this life on earth.

Times of sadness and sorrow affect everyone, and it does not imply a lack of faith to allow tears to flow during periods of grief, separation, or loss. Jesus cried at the tomb of his friend, Lazarus, and wept over the sins of the city of Jerusalem. Suppressing or denying such feelings can be extremely detrimental to our emotional and physical health. We should admit to ourselves and to the Father any sadness, pain, or grief in our hearts and invite his Spirit to bring us joy in the midst of it.

Nevertheless, to constantly remain in a state of sorrow is contrary to the scriptural injunction: "A glad heart is excellent medicine, a spirit depressed wastes the bones away" (Prv

17:22). When we willingly admit our pain to the Lord, he infuses it with the gentleness of his compassion and love. In John's Gospel, Jesus spoke to the disciples about his death: "you are sad now, but I shall see you again, and your hearts will be full of joy, and that joy no one shall take from you" (Jn 16:22).

The joy Jesus promises is connected with seeing him again, a promise fulfilled after his resurrection. Most of us can understand the happiness created by the return of Jesus if we reflect on our own reunions with loved ones after a long absence. Although Jesus is not appearing in the same way today, he still desires to fill us with joy when we ask him to spiritually walk with us. "Remain in my love.... so that my own joy may be in you and your joy be complete" (Jn 15:10).

Jesus makes clear in this passage that the joy he brings is more than any earthly happiness; it is his own joy flowing from his own spirit. This joy is a gift we can expect when we put our trust in him and agree to remain in his presence every moment of life.

As a speaker at many charismatic gatherings, I frequently observe the gift of joy permeating conference participants and infusing them with new life, renewal, and rebirth. Entering the presence of God and trusting in his mercy always generates a sense of excitement, wonder, and awe. We begin to feel sorrow, grief, and pain departing as Jesus grants us his own joy. This supernatural gift of life is much greater than our feeble attempts to create joy with parties and other festivities.

My area of Florida has advertisements for happy hour in nearly all the local bars, lounges, and restaurants. In theory, this period of time is calculated to bring people happiness through half-priced drinks and hot hors d'oeuvres. In reality it often creates road hazards, hangovers, and broken homes. A great deal of money is spent in our society to make leisure time enjoyable, but true joy only comes through a faith relationship with the Trinity.

The joy which flows through intimate communion with God is a gift in the midst of overwhelming difficulties or tragedies. Because it comes from God and not self-effort, it doesn't leave during periods of poverty, illness, or grief. I recall ministering to a woman whose husband had been killed in an auto accident, leaving her with three small children. We prayed together in the hospital emergency room and asked Jesus to bless her with the gifts she most needed to assist during the funeral and burial. She was so radiant and joy-filled at the cemetery that many felt she was drugged with tranquilizers or denying the reality of the moment, but Jesus gave his joy to strengthen her when she most needed it. Later, when she was better able to handle the pain, we spent much time talking and praying about the grief and loneliness of her situation.

As I am writing this meditation, Florida is experiencing the threat of another hurricane sitting fifty miles off the Gulf Coast and 120 mph winds threaten to blow the city of Clearwater away. Our house is filled with Christian friends who had to evacuate homes and who came to stay with us because our home is on high ground. We have spent several hours singing hymns, praising the Lord, and rejoicing in his saving grace. The weather outside is full of wind, torrential rains, and darkness, but we are experiencing a gift of joy from the Lord.

Paul wrote to the Corinthians: "We are in difficulties on all sides, but never cornered; we see no answer to our problems, but never despair . . ." (2 Cor 4:8). God will grant the oil of gladness to all who call upon his name as long as we remain in his love.

*

Dear Jesus, most of the time it is easier to talk to you about my sorrows than my joys because I am often more aware of pain and unhappiness. But I realize that you promised to give me your own joy to flood my being with new life. Forgive me for the times I fail to appropriate this gift and prefer to wallow in negativity. I believe you want me to be happy because "the joy of the Lord is my strength." Give me courage and confidence to continue the journey of faith. Thank you for this marvelous gift of joy which renews my spirit and brings hope for the future.

TWENTY-FOUR

Faith Means Intercession

Pray all the time, asking for what you need, praying in the spirit on every possible occasion. Never get tired of staying awake to pray for all the saints. (Eph 6:18)

CHRISTIANS OFTEN FIND IT EASIER to have faith for others than for themselves. We may personally feel unworthy of God's graces or consider our particular needs too insignificant for God's attention. We have a tendency to measure the Father's infinite capacity for caring with our finite capabilities and to assume his heart isn't big enough to take care of everything asked of him.

However, Paul reminds us, "my God will fulfill all your needs in Christ Jesus, as lavishly as only God can" (Phil 4:19). The Father desires us to come to him with every detail of our lives; nothing is small or insignificant to him.

Trust in divine providence can be generated through our willingness to reach out and pray for others. Repeatedly the early Christian church was encouraged to pray for one another. The letter of James instructs the sick to send for the elders of the church who "must anoint him with oil in the name of the Lord and pray over him. The prayer of faith will save the sick man and the Lord will raise him up again" (Jas 5:14-15). As we exercise the prayer of faith for others and observe the ways in which God responds to these petitions, our own level of trust begins to rise.

Recently I spoke at a large charismatic conference and led the group to invite the Lord's anointing on their hands for the gift of healing. One woman later told me she left the conference with a new awareness of God's power to heal through her prayers. She stopped at the hospital to visit a young neighbor who was comatose from an auto accident. She prayed for him, asking Jesus to heal the traumas in his body, and within a few minutes he began to return to consciousness. This experience did much to heighten the woman's trust relationship with the Father.

Occasionally a person's faith level is nearly non-existent, and he or she may need to rely on the faith of another during a time of illness or tragedy. Scripture narrates the story of a paralyzed man whose four friends lowered him on a stretcher through a roof, placing him at the feet of Jesus. "Seeing their faith he said, 'My friend, your sins are forgiven you'" (Lk 5:20). It appears the stricken man was devoid of belief in Jesus, yet the Lord healed him through the faith of his friends; "seeing their faith," the man's sins were forgiven and his body made whole.

People who have been physically ill for a long time, or who have experienced much rejection, or who have a very poor self-image, often don't believe God cares about them. They find it very difficult to approach the Lord with their needs and will often rationalize this attitude by saying, "God helps those who help themselves." The truth is, Jesus Christ came to help those who couldn't help themselves. There are many areas of life which we are powerless to change, but the mercy of God will be poured out upon us if we but ask for it.

We should be humble enough to invite others to pray for us and not be ashamed to admit our needs. Conversely, we ought to be willing to pray for others even though we are not completely healed in body, mind, or spirit. Such total wholeness will only come in the next life; all of us are wounded healers in one degree or another. Reaching out to relieve another's suffering can bring us much reward. Last year a woman attended a healing mass where she received communion for her mother's impaired hearing. The mother's hearing was restored, but the daughter was also healed of a severe heart problem which she hadn't even mentioned in her petition. Exercising the prayer of faith for others can do much to develop our own trust in God.

*

Merciful Lord, please make me a channel of faith so others can be touched by your loving care. Let me be willing to put aside my own needs as I invite you to heal those who are suffering physical, spiritual, or emotional problems. Teach me to be a source of faith for others so my own trust in you might be strengthened. If I am in need of prayer, help me courageously to ask another to intercede for me and not to think my needs are too insignificant. Thank you for allowing me the privilege of being an intercessor, for all healing ultimately comes through you, with you, and in you.

TWENTY-FIVE

Faith Means Believing without Seeing

For our knowledge is imperfect and our prophesying is imperfect;
but once perfection comes, all imperfect things will disappear. . . .
Now we are seeing a dim reflection in a mirror; but then we shall
be seeing face to face. The knowledge that I have now is imperfect;
but then I shall know as fully as I am known. (1 Cor 13:9-12)

FAITH ISN'T BASED ON FEELINGS but on a belief in God which transcends our finite minds. As the writer of the letter to the Hebrews so eloquently expressed it, "Only faith can guarantee the blessings that we hope for, or prove the existence of the realities that at present remain unseen" (Heb 11:1).

We can have faith in God and still feel empty, uncertain, or anxious about a situation because faith is not based on feelings but on actions. We are hopeful that God's kingdom is already revealed through Jesus Christ but it presently remains unseen and is therefore something we hold onto through our acts of trust in him.

Sometimes we accuse ourselves of lacking faith because we seek answers from the Lord and at the same time, we experience doubts or fears. Mother Angelica, the Abbess of Our Lady of the Angels Monastery in Alabama, defines faith as a "queasy feeling in the pit of your stomach"! The Lord has greatly used this woman in establishing the world's first Catholic cable television network, yet she seldom experiences feelings of euphoria when she steps out in faith to do God's will. "Most of the time I'm not the least bit sure of myself, but walk each step of the way in fear and trembling," Mother says. "Whenever anyone asks me how I discern whether or not a course of action is the will of God, I tell them to ask me a year from now, and I'll be able to know by the outcome." To walk in faith is often a labor of love with little consolation because if we had perfect assurance, there would be no need for faith.

The psalmist wrote, "I have faith, even when I say 'I am completely crushed'" (Ps 116:10). We can be reliant on the providence of the Father, yet feel completely weighed down by our situation. There have been many times in my life when I experienced periods of anxiety, particularly when our five children were all teenagers at the same time and I stayed awake waiting for their return from athletic events, school dances, and high school parties. My lips were praising the Lord yet my heart was heavy with concern as I pondered the many dangers of today's society.

It was then helpful to consider that the great man of faith, Paul of Tarsus, experienced similar reactions in watching over the early Christian community: "there is my daily preoccupation: my anxiety for all the churches. When any man has had scruples, I have had scruples with him; when any man is made to fall, I am tortured" (2 Cor 11:28).

Paul didn't equate his faith with his feelings but continued to trust in God despite the inner turmoil which plagued him from time to time. We can know that God is in his holy temple and all is well with the world, but we may not experience an inner conviction of that truth.

The same Paul who sometimes felt anxiety told the church at Philippi, "There is no need to worry; but if there is anything you need, pray for it" (Phil 4:6). Peter reiterated the same theme in his epistle, "unload all your worries on to him, since he is looking after you" (1 Pt 5:7).

Faith can be exercised by calling upon the Lord's love and mercy in the midst of fears and doubts. We trust in God by yielding our negativity to him, by willingly admitting we are frightened of the outcome of our situation. Coming to the Father with every concern demonstrates much faith because we are clearly showing that we trust in him in spite of fearful feelings.

People often comment on my seeming confidence in addressing large gatherings, but they would be very surprised to know the amount of tension I experience prior to any public speaking engagement. As time goes on, I've become better able to present a "calm, cool, and collected" personality, but the inner struggles continue. If I didn't have faith in God, I would never get up in front of a microphone, but many years of public ministry have shown me that the Father has never allowed me to be embarrassed, mute, or stupid during a speaking engagement, so I refuse to be victimized by my feelings. However, I still make a practice of telling the Lord how I feel and I ask him to relieve the anxieties so he may be glorified through my words. He knows me even better than I know myself, so it's foolish to try to pretend otherwise.

Faith in God never guarantees total freedom from doubt, but life experiences give us the opportunities to walk through doubt, secure in the knowledge that he walks right beside us.

*

Heavenly Father, please help me to keep my eyes on you and not on myself, for my heart is sometimes fearful and anxious about many things. I want to trust you through all the difficulties, trials, and sufferings of my life. Fill my inner being with your presence, let your love give me courage to persevere in spite of doubts. Jesus, strengthen me to resist giving up when I don't feel faith-filled. Grant me hope in the realities of your kingdom which is not yet seen, for I trust in your invisible union with me.

TWENTY-SIX

Faith Means Witnessing

The word, that is the faith that we proclaim, is very near to you,
it is on your lips and in your heart. If your lips confess that Jesus
is Lord and if you believe in your heart that God raised him from
the dead, then you will be saved. By believing from the heart you
are made righteous; by confessing with your lips you are
saved. (Rom 10:8-10)

PAUL EXHORTED HIS FRIEND TIMOTHY to "proclaim the message and, welcome or unwelcome, insist on it" (2 Tm 4:1). He wanted Timothy to understand the importance of sharing his faith with others so they in turn might become believers. In the economics of God's heavenly kingdom, the more we give away our faith, the more we have for ourselves.

Jesus commissioned us in the power of his Holy Spirit to be witnesses throughout the world to the "ends of the earth." We were to tell everyone the good news of salvation because it is a gift to be shared by all mankind. Our own dependence on Jesus Christ as Savior and Lord increases when we share this truth with others.

Telling another person about our faith experiences is a potent form of evangelization because faith is highly contagious when presented with conviction, enthusiasm, and sensitivity. Paul wrote to the Roman church, "they will not ask for him unless they believe in him, and they will not believe in him unless they have heard of him, and they will not hear of him unless they get a preacher. . . . faith comes from what is preached, and what is preached comes from the word of Christ" (Rom 10:14-17).

At a recent charismatic conference a young man told the story of release from drug addiction through the power of Jesus Christ. His testimony moved seventeen persons to come forward to accept freedom from sin and to receive new life in the Lord.

Sometimes we find it difficult to talk about our relationship with Jesus because we are not comfortable exposing our spiritual life; however, true faith in God requires a willingness to tell of his actions in our lives. Jesus stated, "If anyone declares himself for me in the presence of men, I will declare myself for him in the presence of my Father in heaven. But the one who disowns me in the presence of men, I will disown in the presence of my Father in heaven" (Mt 10:32). Thus telling others about Jesus brings abundant blessings upon the speaker as well as the listener.

Paul was given renewed trust in the Lord when Timothy returned from Thessalonica with good news from the believers. He later wrote to them, "Your faith has been a great comfort to us in the middle of our own troubles and sorrows; now we can breathe again, as you are still holding firm in the Lord" (1 Thes 3:7-8). Even those who are fully committed to their Christianity become edified by hearing another's story of trusting in the Father.

One of the most fruitful aspects of the prayer group movement is the time allotted for personal witnessing by the members. Sharing faith experiences can build a strong foundation of trust within us to undergird us when trials and difficulties arise.

"If anyone acknowledges that Jesus is the Son of God, God lives in him, and he in God" (1 Jn 4:15). When we admit we are followers of Jesus Christ, we open our spirit to a greater awareness of the Father's love. We begin to know he does live in us when we willingly acknowledge his presence.

My father-in-law was an Assembly of God pentecostal believer who constantly witnessed about the power of God working in his life, often to the consternation of his daughter, Rose. Every afternoon Paul would walk to the neighborhood barber shop where he would share the good news of Jesus Christ to anyone who cared to listen. "Daddy, those men don't want you bothering them when they're getting haircuts," Rose would plead with him. But Paul never heeded her words and, until the day before his death at the age of eighty-nine, he continued to share the message. At the funeral, Rose was amazed at the numbers of men who told her the importance of her father's influence through his preaching in the barber shop. Even the barber thanked her for having such a wonderful father who wasn't afraid to talk about his faith. "He never drove away my customers; most were interested to hear what he had to say." The young pastor of the church Paul attended said, "Your father was my advisor on the Bible and all spiritual matters. I never knew anyone so firm in his faith and so willing to share it with others."

Witnessing is accomplished by our words but also by the example of the kind of life we lead. If we profess to believe in Jesus Christ, then our actions should bear witness to his presence; "your light must shine in the sight of men, so that, seeing your good works, they may give praise to your Father in heaven" (Mt 5:16). We make a clear statement of trust in God by refusing to behave in ways contrary to his teachings.

A Christian businessman told me of an experience he had when on a business trip. Several of his companions wanted to visit a topless bar and his refusal to join them was met with scorn, until he stated that Jesus Christ lived in his heart and he would never go anywhere offensive to the Lord or to his own wife and children. This simple witness caused all of them to change plans and return to the hotel. When he retired from the company, dozens of fellow employees privately told him how much his Christian behavior had influenced their lives. Until that moment he had not realized how much his actions were proclaiming faith in Jesus Christ.

Each of us is called to be an ambassador of the kingdom of God through our words and actions which shine forth like candles in the darkness of the world.

*

Holy Spirit of God, please give me the courage to admit my faith in the Father, in Jesus Christ, and in you. Help me to willingly speak to others about your presence in my life, telling them of the special place you have in my heart. Let me not overlook any opportunity to share my faith with others. Give me the words which will inspire deeper trust in you, so I may ever be a source of life to those who hear me. Let my actions always proclaim your goodness so that by seeing my good works, others will give praise to your holy name. Thank you for the privilege of witnessing to your presence; if my lips confess that Jesus is Lord and I believe in my heart that God raised him from the dead, I will be saved.

TWENTY-SEVEN

Faith Means History

All these died in faith, before receiving any of the things that had been promised, but they saw them in the far distance and welcomed them, recognizing that they were only strangers and nomads on earth. People who use such terms about themselves make it quite plain that they are in search of their real homeland . . . their heavenly homeland. (Heb 11:13-16)

THE BOOK OF HEBREWS has a lengthy discourse on the heroes of faith who teach us the true meaning of trust in God. In the eleventh chapter, the writer describes many of the men and women who relied on the Lord, who did not fail to respond to their trust.

Abel offered God the appropriate sacrifice and was rewarded; Noah was obedient to Yahweh's command to build an ark, thus saving his family and creation from extinction; Abraham listened to God and abandoned his homeland and became the father of a great nation; Moses trusted the Lord's guidance and brought freedom to the Israelites. "Remember your leaders . . . imitate their faith," the author reminds us (Heb 13:7), because remembering engenders faith.

Recalling the Father's interactions with his people encourages us to turn to him with the same expectancy. The Hebrews constantly told and re-told the stories of their experiences with Yahweh, especially when they were faced with great obstacles which required renewed faith. Their faith level grew as they reminded one another of the Lord's power, promises, and protections.

The book of Judith tells of such an experience when the Israelites became dispirited because the Assyrians had surrounded them for thirty-four days, cutting off all lines of retreat. Every water jar was empty, their wells were drying up, the children were dying, the people were collapsing in the streets and gateways of the town. They demanded Uzziah, the chief of the town, to surrender all into the hands of Holofernes and his army; "after all we should be much better off as their booty than we are now; no doubt we shall be enslaved, but at least we shall be alive and not see our little ones dying before our eyes" (Jud 7:21).

Word of this despondency reached Judith, a Hebrew widow who spent her days in prayer and fasting. She was greatly respected by the Jews because she so devoutly worshipped the Lord. She sharply reprimanded the people for their lack of trust in God: "Let us rather give thanks to the Lord our God who, as he tested our ancestors is now testing us. Remember how he treated Abraham, all the ordeals of Isaac, all that happened to Jacob in Syrian Mesopotamia while he kept the sheep of Laban, his mother's brother. For all these ordeals were intended by him to search their hearts . . ." (Jud 8:25-27).

Judith gave the people of God a renewed sense of their history as she recounted the deeds of old and gave them courage to rally around her plan for the defeat of the Assyrians.

Each of us has a history of relating to God which carries wonderful stories of the Father's victorious working in our lives. Prayer groups should have a secretary who records the many answers to prayer received by the group so they can reflect on these events during moments of weak faith, doubts, or fears. Our personal history of salvation and the history of each charismatic community is an ongoing chapter of the book of Acts being demonstrated in contemporary society.

The Catholic Church provides a type of remembering by assigning feast days to honor the saints who have been canonized, and we can gain much insight into faith by reflecting on the ways these men and women related to God. They illustrate what we also are to become through relying on the Lord.

Many of the saints can teach us the importance of obedience, self-sacrifice, and compassion as we read about their struggles and try to emulate their response to life's challenges. For me, St. Elizabeth Seaton is a model of faith who gives a rich example for women to follow. I undoubtedly identify with her in several areas—wife, mother of five children, servant of the Lord no matter what the price. She personally encountered many sorrows in her family, yet steadfastly clung to Jesus Christ as her rock and refuge. She was criticized by her family and friends for converting to Catholicism, but she did not allow their persecutions to keep her from doing what she felt God was calling her to do.

Whenever I become overwhelmed with too many responsibilities, I recall the obstacles she faced in establishing a school system and forming a religious community which survives to this day. St. Elizabeth is but one of the countless saints who can show us the way to our personal sanctity. Reading about their lives, especially in books written by biographers who present their struggles with human weakness, can be most beneficial for growth in faith in the same way that the Israelites gained renewed trust by recalling the heroes of the Jewish tradition.

*

Dear Father, please help me to grow in faith by remembering the many men and women who were not disappointed when they put their trust in you. As I reflect on their lives, give me the courage to follow you as they did. Guide me to read and study those stories of faith in action which will provide a rich source of belief in you so that I may grow in wisdom regarding your divine nature. I want to understand the way you relate to others so I can be more open to your action in my life. "Glory be to him whose power, working in us, can do infinitely more than we can ask or imagine; glory be to him from generation to generation in the church and in Christ Jesus for ever and ever. Amen" (Eph 3).

TWENTY-EIGHT

Faith Means Love

As the Father has loved me, so I have loved you. Remain in my love. If you keep my commandments you will remain in my love, just as I have kept my Father's commandments and remain in his love. I have told you this so that my own joy may be in you and your joy be complete. This is my commandment: love one another, as I have loved you. (Jn 15:9-12)

"IF I HAVE FAITH IN ALL ITS FULLNESS, to move mountains, but without love, then I am nothing at all" (1 Cor 13:2). It is of little use to claim faith and trust in the Father if we do not extend love to those around us, for "anyone who fails to love can never have known God, because God is love" (1 Jn 4:8).

It seems strange that a person can have the kind of faith which "moves mountains" and works healing miracles, signs, and wonders yet can still be out of the will of God because he doesn't know how to love. Jesus told the disciples that many would stand before him on the day of judgment reminding him, "Lord, Lord, didn't we work miracles in your name?" And he will tell them to their faces, "I have never known you; away from me you evil men" (Mt 7:23).

Demonstrations of the power of God which do not proceed from love and produce love come under heavy admonition from the Lord. Talking about faith in God and believing in his power to save without showing actions of love toward family, friends, and coworkers will bring only emptiness and sadness to the spirit. Sometimes I have come away from healing services with a heavy heart because there was so little of God's love demonstrated by the leadership, and although many persons claimed physical healings, there was much disappointment in the hearts of those who were not healed during the service. God's power should always be permeated with his love so everyone feels closer to the Lord, even if total healing is not accomplished.

At a recent healing service in Brisbane, Australia, a woman with bone cancer shared her feelings following the prayer time. She walked with the aid of a walker and was in extreme pain, but as we asked the healing touch of Jesus to bless her body, she was aware of being bathed in his love. "I realized that this spiritual gift of love was so much more important than my physical healing," she said. She still needed to use the walker, though the pain was somewhat decreased, but her face was radiant with happiness for she knew she was loved.

Hunger for love prompts all kinds of destructive behavior, i.e., drug abuse, immorality, and workaholism. The heart cries out for the answers but often seeks the wrong solution, for, as St. Augustine said, "Our hearts will never be at rest until they rest in you, O Lord." Only union with the Father can truly fill the emptiness so common to humanity. He is a God of love, and he desires to bring us love more than we can ask for or imagine.

Paul's letter to the Corinthians contains a long list of spiritual gifts which are well known to most Christians— healing, miracles, prophecy, and tongues are all mentioned as important tools for victorious living. But when Paul instructs the church concerning the gift of love, he gives a lengthy discourse on its characteristics (1 Cor 13). I often use this passage from Scripture as an examination of conscience regarding my exercise of love. Whenever Paul writes "love is always kind" or "love is never jealous," I substitute my name for the word "love" and ask the Lord to reveal ways I fail to act in a loving way to those around me.

I believe when my time of judgment arrives, the Father will not ask me how many were healed through my prayers, nor will he take into account the number of books I wrote, but he will ask me how well I loved. I wear a ring on my finger which constantly reminds me of this mission, for it contains the words of Jesus, "Love one another, as I have loved you" (Jn 15:12). Remaining true to this commandment is my most challenging and rewarding endeavor.

The Lord provides us with training in the school of love by placing unlovable persons into our lives so we can practice the gift of love. He told the disciples, "If you love those who love you, what thanks can you expect? Even sinners love those who love them.... Instead, love your enemies and do good.... You will have a great reward" (Lk 6:34-35). We can expect to have at least one person in our life who rubs us the wrong way, makes us irritated, or doesn't respond as we would like but who provides ample opportunity for us to learn to love the unlovable.

Jean Vanier, the founder of L'Arch communities throughout the world which care for the mentally and physically handicapped, states he prays for one difficult individual to dwell in each house of the apostolate, so the coordinators can learn how to love more fully. Most of us don't dare to ask for such an opportunity to obtain graces because we already have such persons in our lives. Exercising the gift of love is a sure way to live in unity with the Father.

John was known as the beloved disciple because there appeared to be a particularly close relationship between Jesus and John. The gospel he wrote and his three letters to the early church are filled with references to love. It is said that he lived to a very old age and was very feeble and had to be carried from village to village to proclaim the good news. Toward the end of his time on earth, John's message had been reduced to only five words, "Little children, love one another." This admonition is as valid today as it was nearly 2000 years ago. Faith in God cannot be separate from love.

*

Dear Father of Love, deepen my faith in you by bathing me in your tender, loving care. Immerse me in the warmth of your presence and allow me to know how very special I really am to you. Let this awareness spill over into the world around me that I may love others as you are loving me. Help me to love even those who do not love me in return, as I recall the words of Jesus to do good to those who wound me. You yourself are kind to the "ungrateful and the wicked"; may I seek to imitate your divine nature in all my relationships.

TWENTY-NINE

Faith Means a Gift

So far then we have seen that, through our Lord Jesus Christ, by faith we are judged righteous and at peace with God, since it is by faith and through Jesus that we have entered this state of grace in which we boast about looking forward to God's glory . . . . we are filled with joyful trust in God, through our Lord Jesus Christ, through whom we have already gained our reconciliation.
(Rom 5:1-2, 11)

THE VARIOUS ASPECTS OF FAITH outlined in this book can help the Christian believer to reach higher levels of trust in the heavenly Father. Each of us can develop a faith relationship with God by taking time to incorporate wholesome behavior and attitudes into our daily lives. Such willingness to draw closer to the Lord opens the mind, heart, body, and spirit to greater awareness of the Father's goodness, mercy, and love.

Although faith can be stimulated through spiritual exercises, it ultimately remains a gift from God which can be appropriated through prayerfully seeking, knocking, and asking. Whenever we encounter a situation which requires trust in God's providence and we are unable to have an appropriate faith response, we can invite him to gift our spirit with an infusion of grace to believe in his power to bring about the best resolution.

When the Lord began to speak about a center for healing in

the Clearwater, Florida, area, I felt uncertain it could ever become a reality. The obstacles were great, finances were unavailable, no appropriate facility could be located, but three of us, Margaret Leeseberg, Diane Brown, and myself, continued to meet every Tuesday morning to intercede for this project. As we sought the Father's will, a gift of faith began to emerge and brought with it a determination to carry out this mission no matter what impediments stood in the way. We still didn't have land or money, but we knew it was going to happen. This gift of faith enabled us to pray with conviction for nearly two years until Our Lady of Divine Providence House of Prayer became a reality. The many other occasions when such a gift became manifested in our hearts can only be attributed to the intervention of the Father who understands the weaknesses of our humanity and infuses it with the power of his divinity.

Fr. Michael Scanlan, the President of the Franciscan University of Steubenville, Ohio, states he often wrestles with a lack of faith concerning the needs of the college and the burden of his responsibilities for the students and faculty. At such times the Holy Spirit speaks to his heart, "Michael, do you know how far beyond your resources you have already gone?" With that word, the Father inspires Fr. Scanlan with a fresh outpouring of the gift of faith which sustains him through another time of crisis.

Mary, the mother of Jesus, was given a supernatural ability to trust in God when she said "yes" to accepting the motherhood of Jesus Christ. Her cousin, Elizabeth, confirmed this by saying, "blessed is she who believed that the promise made her by the Lord would be fulfilled" (Lk 1:45). Mary's belief in the Father's power to watch over her and the child within her were obvious to Elizabeth even before Mary told her of the angel's visit. Whenever the Father requires us to do something for him, he likewise grants us the necessary gift of faith when we ask for it. "If you then, who are evil, know how to give your children what is good, how much more will the heavenly Father give the Holy Spirit to those who ask him!" (Lk 11:13). One of the gifts of the Spirit is faith, and when we prayerfully petition the Father, he will grant it to us in abundance.

Courageously we invite God's Spirit to grant us all we need to continue the spiritual journey which leads to eternal life.

"Through your faith, God's power will guard you until the salvation which has been prepared is revealed at the end of time."
(1 Pt 1:5)

*

Eternal Father, I praise you for blessing me with faith in your Holy Trinity. I believe in salvation through the cross of Jesus Christ and acknowledge him as Savior and Lord. I proclaim your Holy Spirit as a bearer of your powerful gifts and seek a gift of faith to sustain me in times when I experience weakness in my ability to trust in you. Thank you for recognizing my need for a renewal of faith as you deepen my trust through challenging life experiences. Enable me to respond to your presence by giving me the courage to follow your commandments and yield to your will. I sincerely desire to know you, love you, and serve you in this life and in the world to come.

Other Books of Interest
from Servant Books

Let the Fire Fall
By Michael Scanlan

The story of how the power of the Holy Spirit revolutionized the life of Father Mike Scanlan. *$7.95*

The Disciplines of a Disciple
By John Bertolucci

America's best-known Catholic evangelist shares what he has learned about the challenges and rewards of living as a disciple of Jesus Christ. *$5.95*

Only a Prayer Away
By John Guest

A month-long course in prayer, filled with scriptural teaching, personal examples, and suggestions for further reflection and prayer. *$6.95*

Available at your Christian Bookstore or from:
**Servant Publications • Dept. 209 • P.O. Box 7455
Ann Arbor, Michigan 48107**
Please include payment plus $1.25 for postage.
*Send for our FREE catalog of Christian
books, music, and cassettes.*